The Road to Ruins

A Lifetime Pursuit of Puzzles and Predicaments from Colorado's Custer County to Peru

Gary Ziegler

The Road to Ruins

A Lifetime Pursuit of Puzzles and Predicaments from Colorado's Custer County to Peru

Gary Ziegler

Filter Press, LLC
www.FilterPressBooks.com

The Road to Ruins: A Lifetime Pursuit of Puzzles and Predicaments from Colorado's Custer County to Peru

Filter Press, LLC
Westcliffe, Colorado
https://www.FilterPressBooks.com/

*To all the amazing people I have met over the years.
Thanks for all the memories!*

And to my wife, Amy Finger Ziegler

Contents

Foreword by Hugh Thomson
Exploring the Vilcabamba with Gary Ziegler

The Peruvian Vilcabamba, the mountainous area to the west of both Cusco and Machu Picchu, remained unexplored until the 20th Century, both because of its geographical isolation and a lack of interest. The Vilcabamba became difficult to travel in during the height of the Sendero Luminoso years in the 1990s, and it was not until 2002 that interest in the area was reawakened with the discovery of a hill-top Inca site on Cerro Victoria by a National Geographic team led by Peter Frost and Gary Ziegler—the author of this book.

This was followed in the same year by the discovery of another site by Ziegler and myself called Cota Coca, which lies in the lower Yanama valley and had been concealed for many years because the sides of that valley have collapsed.

In 2003, another much larger Thomson–Ziegler Research Expedition, this time supported by the Royal Geographical Society, used thermal imaging cameras to fly over the cloud-forest and find the outlines of stone buildings beneath the vegetation. They were accompanied by the archeoastonomer Kim Malville and anthropologist Tom Zuidema. The main Inca site under investigation was called Llactapata—appropriately one of the very sites Bingham had first reported partially on, in 1912. As with Espíritu Pampa, Llactapata was found to be far larger than Bingham had initially realised and contained what was later confirmed to be an Inca observatory and sun-temple.

The above is a short summary only of the main expeditions that have been made into the Vilcabamba. The reader may well ask why discoveries are still being made there when the rest of the world is so well mapped? It is partly because the Vilcabamba is such a dense quadrant of twisting river canyons and thick cloud-forests, making it easy to pass within ten feet of a ruin and miss it.

Both for aesthetic and strategic reasons, the Incas chose to build on remote, isolated sites, as even the most casual visitor to Machu Picchu can observe. They also often built settlements in sectors scattered at different levels on a hillside, so that while one sector may have been found, others remain hidden.

All these factors mean that it is highly likely more ruins will be found in the years to come. The Vilcabamba has by no means given up all its secrets.

This is by way of being an introduction to the Vilcabamba, Gary Ziegler and to a certain extent myself, in as much as it explains how I have come to know him.

But I like to go back to our very first encounter in around 2000 when we made contact by the relatively new Internet once I realised we had mutual interests.

We met at Huancacalle which in those days lay at the end of the road before it petered out into mule tracks and descended to the jungle below. It lies very close to the old capital of the Incas in exile, Vitcos, and the great carved sacred stone of 'Chuquipalta' or 'Yurak Rumi', often called 'The White Rock' as it was by me in my book of the same name. There was a small hostel there, set up by the Cobos family who were guides, and much used by explorers. It was spartan, but it had a shower and more importantly it had beer.

It was a long journey to get there and night had fallen by the time I arrived. Leaning against the doorway to meet me was Gary's tall, rangy figure. In his Stetson and breeches, he looked as if he might have stepped off a Colorado ranch — as indeed he had. Gary was a true *vaquero*, a cowboy, who was part owner of a hundred head of horses back in the States and mixed his exploring with ranch management. In fact Gary mixed his exploring with just about everything else in the Tom Sawyer logbook of jobs for active boys: over sixty years of enjoyably hard living, he had worked as a photographer, mountain guide, geologist and yacht handler.

Once, after a trip exploring the Vilcabamba, Gary had rolled up at a local train station, left his hired horse—he insisted on riding everywhere—and rolled wearily into the carriage with his companions. The Quechua Indians on the train gave them a wide berth, but Gary and his crew were too tired to worry about what might be wrong. Finally one Indian sidled nervously up to Gary: "Excuse me, *Señor*, but I've been talking with my friends and—are you Clint Eastwood?"

Over some vicious vodka martinis that Gary mixed (I learnt later he never travelled anywhere without a bottle of vodka and some green olives), we swapped stories.

Gary, like me, didn't like the Amazon much. "I worked in intelligence in South-east Asia during Vietnam, and I tell you that was enough jungle for me. Used to go out on night patrols with infra-red vision to pick the enemy out with. Then we'd get those suckers. I tell you, being in the army is fun—at least in wartime. In peacetime it's kind of dull."

He had climbed most of the major peaks in the area and many of the minor ones. "I like those little suckers," he said, "the little insignificant peaks that no one else is ever going to bother with. Most have never been climbed before. Hell, most don't even have a name."

We had teamed up to visit the site of Inca Wasi, so we headed back down the valley a little to the small village of Yupanqa and started to load up the mules we had hired. As I knew from years of experience, this was not as straightforward as it might have seemed.

The procedure for loading mules is similar to that which an elderly aunt of mine adopts when going on holiday. First the muleteers lay out all the bundles on the grass and move them around until they look deceptively ordered and graded. Then these bundles are packed into saddle-bags and onto the mules (in my aunt's case, suitcases). Like her, the muleteers will invariably decide that everything is in the wrong place and must be taken out so that the process can be started all over again. Meanwhile at least one mule will have got bored and absconded over the horizon.

Experienced *arrieros* can spin this process out for hours. We were lucky and got off that same morning. For our later and larger expeditions, we established the tradition of having a 'vodka mule' with us, loaded with a crate of Stolichnaya from the Cross Keys pub in Cusco—and for some trips, we indulgently made it two crates, telling ourselves this would not then unbalance the mule.

As we started up into the rugged, igneous peaks of the Puncuyoc hills and looked back, we could see why Vitcos was such a convenient centre for the Incas in their exile – it was the hub of a wheel, with spokes extending not only into the Puncuyoc, but away towards the jungle at Old Vilcabamba and up the Choquetecarpa pass towards Choquequirao: beyond were various areas around Pumasillo and Arma that remain under-explored—but were already attracting our attention. In the centre Vitcos rose up, a natural location for Manco's sons to use as his successors reviewed their domains as Lords of the Vilcabamba.

As befitted a cowboy, Gary had made sure that we had riding horses for the trip. This was a novelty for me, and not a wholly welcome one. I was used to keeping two feet firmly on the ground. While the idea of occasionally mounting up and letting the horse do the work was agreeable, I suspected that the narrow, overgrown paths wouldn't allow for much maneuvering.

We set off up the hill at a ferocious rate, made harder by the fact that while the trail was initially surprisingly good, Gary suggested we lead rather than ride the horses. I asked a little petulantly what the point of having the horses was.

"Exercise," replied Gary laconically.

My own horse sensed I was not a natural horseman, so I had to pull it up most of the way. Just when I was regretting my lack of fitness, the others started to talk about "running up the mountain, because walking's *so* boring." They even had trainers packed for the eventuality. I put my best foot forward and thought of the vodka martini at the end of the day.

We rose above the cloud-line and had a spectacular view of the Pumasillo mountain range rising up ahead. Mount Pumasillo has a curious characteristic: despite being 20,000 feet high, it is so shielded by a host of lesser mountains as to be completely invisible to the surrounding valleys and villages. Only when some distance away does it reveal itself (it was not even accurately put on the map until 1956).

I sat up late with Gary at camp that night, talking about previous expeditions. I quickly realised that Gary had enormous energy for archaeological exploration and an instinct for finding the spoors of long-forgotten Inca roads and buildings that came from thirty years of hunting them down. He also brought an immense range of knowledge to his exploring, from geology to obscure forms of cattle disease, fueled by an obsessive drive that had kept him coming back again long after most men would have hung up their boots.

"The thing is guys like us are all a little off-centre," he told me. "Explorers have to be. Otherwise we just wouldn't do it."

This book is proof of Gary's endless, ranging curiosity, and his capacity to ask the right questions. I greatly value our long friendship which in the years since that first encounter has been very fruitful, with many wonderful expeditions into those mountains—and plenty of dry martinis at the end of each day.

Hugh Thomson, 2026
Winner of the Wainwright Prize and
one of Britain's leading travel writers

Introduction by Amy Finger Ziegler

In 1971, my family bought property three miles from where Gary Ziegler, the year before, in 1970, bought the first 350 acres of what he named Bear Basin Ranch. For several summers, my older brothers and I lived at our small property in Cristo Vista, completing construction on a geodesic dome. Gary says he remembers seeing me at the "Finger Dome"when he came to dinners my brothers threw there in the 1970s.

Eventually, I stopped in at Bear Basin Ranch and arranged for a day horseback ride in exchange for helping Gary put up hay in his meadow. He was living the life of an 1880s homesteader, growing triticale (a hybrid of wheat) for animal feed, growing his own vegetables, and using firewood as his sole source of heat. His success with weekend riding groups came in part from the fact the ranch had no electric power. Visitors loved the kerosene lights and pancakes cooked on an ancient cast-iron wood cook stove.

We rode from the ranch to the Finger Dome and back. Along the way, Gary was talking nonstop about the history of who owned what—a pattern of conversation that persists to this day. Gary enjoys searching history for how things came

Amy and Gary

to be.

In May 1980, I stopped at the ranch again and asked if he needed help. "Yes! I need help," he said. "You could move into the cabin next to the corral and get started." I did just that and I never left.

Thirty years later we got married.

Early on Gary introduced me to his favorite places in Mexico and Peru. He had his PhD in archaeology, the perfect field for him. I was swept up in his pursuit of past puzzles. The complexity of the Mexican Revolution. Why did the Inca choose to build where they did? Were there still unsolved puzzles hidden there in the cloud forest?

Every trip seemed to involve a predicament. Gary was very good at solving them and seemed to enjoy problem solving—an aspect of his personality that I think got him through the Vietnam years mentally unscathed.

Gary's gift for enthusiastically recounting history made for fun times for guests around the campfire on the Colorado horse packing trips we operated for the next several decades. Some of our staff might not have been as enthralled since it meant they did the majority of the work while Gary talked. They also didn't believe Gary had done all the things he told stories about.

I knew better.

All of Gary's stories are true. I participated in some of them, and others were confirmed when characters from a story came to visit us and confirmed all the facts. Gary has led a remarkable life, becoming a living Indiana Jones.

As of this writing, Gary is eighty-five and has credibility with everyone he works and lives with. As he ages, he is coming more and more into his own. His memory is still sharp, full of energy and vibrancy.

Gary has an incredible life story, and this compilation of the highlights is not only the real thing but is highly informative, thought-provoking, and fascinating.

His wife and best friend,
Amy Finger Ziegler

CHAPTER 1

The Ziegler Family and My Early History

I entered the scene at St John's Hospital in Salina, Kansas on March 7, 1941. My father, Raymond Francis Ziegler, was the only son of John and Bertha Ziegler. John was a long-time trainman with the Union Pacific Railroad. Bertha was actively involved with women's rights movements, leading a group to Washington DC, in support of obtaining the vote in 1918. My mother, Viola Fern Ziegler, was a daughter of Charles W. and Lillie Frazier. My grandmother Lillie Frazier was a Sherman niece, relating me on that side of the family back to William Tecumseh Sherman. Both Viola and Raymond were born in 1909.

In 1942, I arrived with my folks in Florence, Colorado where my dad, Raymond, took a job editing and printing the local newspaper, *The Florence Citizen*. We soon moved to Hill Field, an army air base at Ogden, Utah, where Raymond trained and worked as a civilian rebuilding and testing damaged B-24s and B-17s.

Following the end of the war, we moved to Manitou

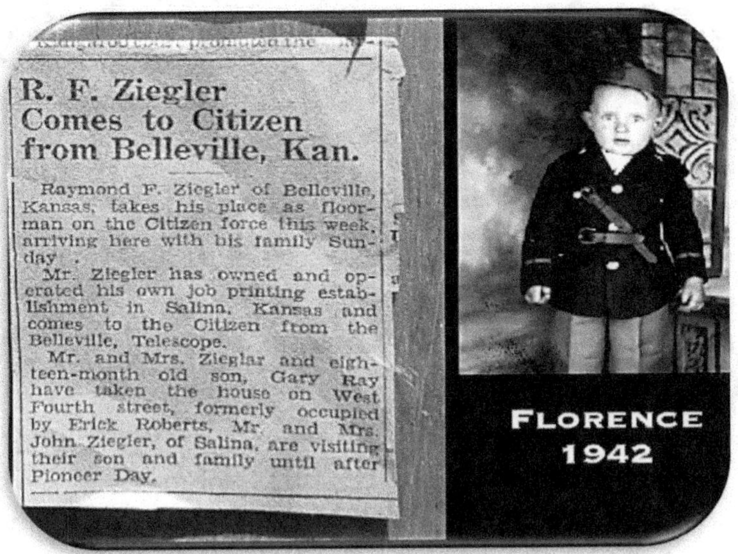

R. F. Ziegler
Comes to Citizen
from Belleville, Kan.

Raymond F. Ziegler of Belleville, Kansas, takes his place as floorman on the Citizen force this week, arriving here with his family Sunday.

Mr. Ziegler has owned and operated his own job printing establishment in Salina, Kansas and comes to the Citizen from the Belleville, Telescope.

Mr. and Mrs. Zieglar and eighteen-month old son, Gary Ray have taken the house on West Fourth street, formerly occupied by Erick Roberts. Mr. and Mrs. John Ziegler, of Salina, are visiting their son and family until after Pioneer Day.

Gary's father joined *The Florence Citizen* in 1942.

Springs. Working as a printer, Ray eventually became a partner in the Out West Printing and Stationary Company in Colorado Springs while forming a small mining company, Ziegler Minerals and Mining.

With his company, my father dabbled in purchasing mining properties in Cripple Creek and elsewhere. Teaming up with local mineral collectors and prospectors, he located productive deposits of collectible minerals and crystals around the Pikes Peak region. As his tag-a-long helper I got a

Gary's mother and Gary at
Royal Gorge, 1942

My father, Raymond Francis Ziegler (left). Revolutionary War hero and first mayor of Cincinnati, Major Johann David Ziegler, one of my ancestors (right).

good early education in the basics of field geological exploration and mineralogy.

In 1948, we moved to a newly built home on North Spruce Street near downtown Colorado Springs. At that time, Colorado Springs was a small city seeped in western heritage, with an acceptance for multiracial populations that went back to early ethnic blending. The area's population included Goodnight's Texas-Mexican cowboys, Chinese and other railroad builders, assorted settlers, miners, Bent's "half-breed" trapper-traders, camping plains tribes, and Buffalo Soldiers of the army's Ninth Calvary.

I started first grade behind an imposing three-story brick structure, Bristol School, on North Walnut Street. The neighborhood formed the eastern edge of what came to be known as the Old West Side. My classmates were a mix of whites, blacks, and a smattering of Hispanics, reflecting the integrated composition of the neighborhood. This was before terms like *Anglo*, *African*, and *Native American* became vogue.

Every day I traveled everywhere safely on a big, fat-tired Schwinn bicycle. I delivered carefully rolled *Gazette Telegraph Newspapers* stuffed in massive canvas handlebar bags. Being tasked with monthly subscription collection, I quickly learned that all did not pay their bills.

Our neighborhood hosted several community notables. Fanny Mae Duncan, proprietor of the famous Cotton Club on West Colorado Avenue, owned a large two-story house, a block away from us on Pine Street. I remember big shiny cars and elegantly attired black gents coming and going from there, and, yes, Fanny did promptly pay her paper subscription.

I went on to attend North Junior High and mingle with a crowd of mainly white kids on the more affluent North Side. It was there that I met classmate Steve Sprague and his historian-author father, Marshall Sprague, who published the definitive work on local history, *Newport in the Rockies*. We both went on to graduate from the last class at Colorado Springs

Gary and his father in front of their 509 Spruce Street home in Colorado Springs, 1948 (left). Gary with his scout master father and Bristol School Troop 4, 1955 (right).

High School before it became Palmer High School.

I sat through courses on physics, earth science, and Latin and played hockey and baseball.

Reaching far back in personal history, several classmates at Colorado Springs High School and I became interested in exploring caves, joining an organization called the National Speleological Society (NSS). This was an early metamorphosis for my education, coupling scientific discovery with wild adventure. Along with technical rock climbing, we utilized weekends to launch explorations of lesser-known Colorado caves. These getaway sorties were a needed relief after struggling through Mrs. Zinn's English class or Dean Moon's chemistry lab experiments and exams during the week.

Close by home we could slip into Manitou's William's Canyon to party and explore Huccacove, a well-known and frequently visited local cave. Although attempts were made to seal it, someone always broke the entrance open again. When I shared my cave memories with an old friend, she shared her own memories with me:

Reminds me of my first and only spelunking experience with you . It must have been Manitou. Remember that narrow sandy rim we had to tread in order to navigate around a deep dark watery pit? That was terrifying to me. And then the stovepipe with 90-degree turn I imagined getting stuck in. Memories very clear, registered in fear as they were, though for you, no doubt, old hat by that point.

High school caver friend Bob Doane and I explored several other local caves. Lower down in Williams Canyon, on the west side of the road, was another interesting cave . After a short walk in from the entrance close to the road, it opened into a very large chamber almost filled by a huge flowing pond. Bob tried an experiment to see where the water went, expecting it to emerge below Manitou in Fountain Creek.

He poured a packet of what I recall was green fluorescein dye into the pond. Unexpectedly, it came out in one of the town's main tourist attraction fountains, causing quite a stir. I recall the story appeared in the several local newspapers of the day, *The Gazette and Telegraph*, *The Free Press*, and probably Manitou's own *Pikes Peak Journal*, operated by the Graham family, friends of my folks. As it turns out, the dyeing of the fountain mystery was never solved.

Ray Ziegler holding a crystal sample at Lake George, Colorado, 1967

Crestone Needle with South Colony Lake in the foreground, located near Westcliffe, Colorado. Crestone Needle's Ellingwood Route is a technical climbing route, also known as Ellingwood Arete. An arete is a sharp, narrow ridge like the one shown.
Wikipedia Image

But then maybe it never happened.

During the summer of 1956, at age fifteen, I ran in the first Pikes Peak Marathon, finishing seventh out of fifteen. My dad was one of the organizers and donated a quartz and amazonite crystal as part of the winners' awards. I ran the marathon again, this time the ascent only, during the fifty-year anniversary of the race in 2006 as a guest of honor. I guess I was the only one they could find alive who had run the Peak in those early years.

Sometime in the mid-1950s, I learned backcountry skiing and began technical rock climbing on the rock towers of nearby Garden of the Gods and North Cheyenne Canyon. An early accomplishment at the age of fourteen was climbing the Ellingwood Arete on the fourteen-thousand-foot Crestone Needle with climbing legend Robert Ormes.

Bob, as he went by, was a family friend and English professor at Colorado College, where my dad lectured part-time for the Geology Department. Being a local and having these connections, I was admitted as a freshman with less than stellar grades from high school. I tried out for the school's famous hockey team but didn't make the cut. Seems I was not Canadian, or so we joked.

CHAPTER 2

High School Caving in Custer County's Marble Mountain Cave

There were several other caves of interest that we explored while I was in high school. One favorite, the name of which I have forgotten, is located in the canyon leading up from William Palmer's Glen Erie Castle complex, north of Garden of the Gods. It was particularly challenging, requiring a rock-climbing approach to gain entrance. I suspect it has long since been sealed.

Another challenging cave closer to Custer County opens in a steep limestone wall near Shelf Road, an old wagon route that runs from Cañon City to Cripple Creek. It was particularly difficult and scary, requiring several hundred feet of crawling and frequent squeezing through very tight places to reach a grotto chamber. The area has become a popular rock-climbing destination in recent times. Driving a herd of long-horn cattle up Shelf Road in the 1990s is a story for another time.

Now to the essence of this story: the mysteries, legends, and explorations associated with Marble Mountain and its assortment of high-altitude cavities, caverns, mining claims, and abandoned camps.

Marble Mountain is a sort of geological anomaly. The bedrock limestone is a fault block created as an isolated remnant of the Pennsylvanian age, the Minturn Formation. It is wedged between differing geomorphic elements of the Sangre de Cristo Formation, extending north and south and forming the Sangre de Cristo Mountains.

A cave system can only be created in a water-soluble material like limestone. The thick, extensive mass of Marble Mountain is unique to the range in offering this environment. Other than a few thin bands of limestone elsewhere unsuitable for cave creation, Marble Mountain presents the only cave possibility.

My involvement with Marble Mountain and its caves goes back to those early caving and climbing years in the late 1950s. My high school classmate Bob Doane and I loaded up camping gear into my "hot rod" 1949 Ford flathead V-8 with NSS

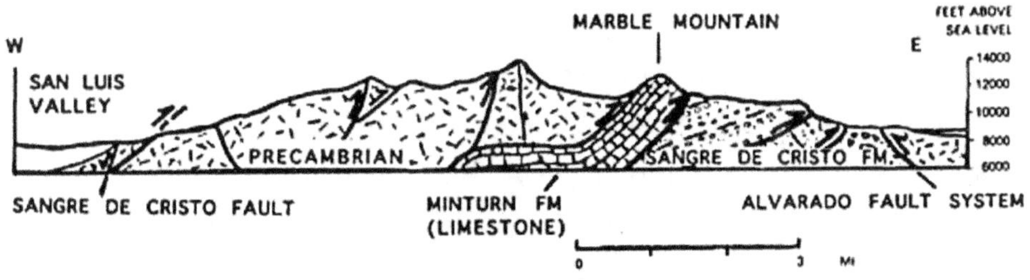

Geology of Marble Mountain
Courtesy of the David A. Lindsey Collection

stickers on the rear window. We bounced up the dusty, rough dirt road over Hardscrabble Pass through Westcliffe and headed south to South Colony Road. Turning off the road, we joined a small NSS group camping at a ranch just before the National Forest near Crystal Falls Creek.

As the youngest and least experienced, Bob and I joined in with considerable awe and trepidation. The next morning, we sorted and helped pack what seemed an excessive amount of equipment. I remember big coils of World War II-vintage, OD green, 7/16-inch braided nylon climbing rope that was in use at the time. There were several canvas bags of rope ladders, a supply of carbide, used in flame illuminating headlamps; and assorted camping supplies. A tough-looking packer, I believe it was Harry Diekmann from the Alvarado Campground, showed up with a string of pack horses to carry all this up Marble Mountain.

By late afternoon, we arrived at a small level meadow just below timberline. This ended the trail for the pack horses. The route on to our objective, Marble Cave (also known as Spanish Cave and La Caverna del Oro), climbed steeply up an eroded gully to a small north-side shelf about one thousand feet above camp. We staggered up this with heavy backpacks the next morning. I was happy that I had learned the valuable mountain rest step. Stretching memory a bit—geez, it has been only sixty-seven years—we may have needed several trips to hump up the equipment needed to explore the deep, downward-plunging cave system.

Finally, equipment in place and team organized, we descended into the cave. Again, from distant memory, the cave opened into a small walk-in tunnel partially blocked by ice. The date must have been sometime in the fall, as ice reportedly closes the passage until then. An unusual item

Location of Marble Cave with respect to Marble Mountain

observed outside the entrance was a painted, badly faded, red Maltese cross.

After some distance, around fifty feet, the passage ended overlooking a broad open pit. The temperature was very cold with a strong upward draft coming from below. With belayers securely anchored above for justifiable roped protection, we had a choice of descending with an uncomfortable carabiner and over-the-shoulder rappel or by climbing down the wobbling, unstable rope ladder. We young hotshot climbers of course chose the rappel without protection.

To shorten the story, we worked several hours daily for a couple of days, exploring and mapping the winding passages. Most of these were almost filled with freezing, downplunging streams. We did have newly designed neoprene diving suits and gloves, which made the work possible.

Our exploration produced the first detailed map and scientific description of Marble Cave. I had a copy of the map and would love to have it for this story. Sadly, it is now lost.

However, the story does go on.

As it turns out, I later visited Marble Mountain and poked around other caves on many occasions, looking at all with a geological and archaeological focus. With our Bear Basin Ranch guide and outfitting business, we visited the area many times over the years, camping at that same high meadow. It gave me a good opportunity to examine the many remnants and remains of past human activity there.

At some point, probably during the Silver Cliff mining boom in the late 1870s, a wagon road was built up to a small mine works close to the camp meadow. A collapsed tunnel and small tailing pile indicate that miners gave it a good try, but the mine eventually failed. Samples from the site indicate that the ore was mainly copper which did not justify the expenses and effort involved. A leveled area nearby probably contained a simple log cabin or canvas tent. The remains from the road are evident. It was the trail up for many years. Other more recent mining claims were staked out nearby but never worked beyond a small prospect hole.

There are a number of small prospect pits on the ridge top east of and near the campsite meadow. These indicate that the area was extensively prospected for likely gold and silver.[1] This was probably motivated by old treasure legends along with general mineral searches prompted by successful mining at nearby Rosita and Silver Cliff.

Before the miners, the area was inhabited mostly by

---

[1] Recently, I came in contact with Anna Barry while she was researching the history of family that had settled on lower Antilope Creek, south of present-day Westcliffe. In 1870, Anna's ancestors had worked the mines there and explored the caves, finding no gold or silver.

visiting summer bands of Mountain Ute. I have collected a few chips of imported obsidian and jasper and a point or two, indicating that on some past occasion, stone tools were made there. As for gold mining, stashed treasure, Spanish explorers, armor-clad skeletons, forts, mysterious monks, and enslaved Ute, one can't mention Marble Cave without including a few historical stories.

The legend of Marble Cave, sometimes called La Caverna del Oro (Cave of Gold), is said to have been passed down from generation to generation by Native Americans. Monks translated the legend, and Spanish explorers eagerly sought to find the gold. In 1541, as the legend goes, three Spanish monks from the Coronado expedition forced Native Americans to extract gold from the cave. Vast amounts of gold were brought forth from the underground passages by the enslaved natives. Brother De la Cruz from the Coronado expedition and a group of Spaniards killed the Indians, loaded up their treasure on pack mules, and fled south back to Mexico.

In 1870, the cave was allegedly rediscovered by Elisha Horn. He claimed to have found an armor-clad skeleton with an arrow in back near the entrance of the cave and next to a painted Maltese cross. In the 1920s, the Colorado Mountain Club and a Forest Service team explored the cave and surrounding area. They are said to have discovered a two-hundred-year-old ladder and a hammer made in the 1600s.

Lower down, hidden in aspen trees, the group supposedly found the ruins of an old fort with arrowheads scattered about. Other explorers are said to have uncovered old items such as a windlass rope, a bucket, a clay jug, and a shovel left by earlier explorers or miners. One group of cavers even claimed to have seen a human skeleton chained by the neck to a wall deep down in the cave.

Fact versus myth in history is sometime very difficult to

determine.[2] All that being said, the mountain's unique high-altitude cave system is a rare and interesting natural phenomenon enhancing our unique mountain community. Myth, mysteries, and legends are enriching aspects of life in the Old West. A visit to the mountain is well worth the effort.

Who knows, maybe Coronado's ghost along with Ute guardian spirits of the sacred landscape still roam the mountainside when the full moon rises.

---

[2] I wrote a story for *The Wet Mountain Tribune* published on November 28, 2024. In the article, called "From Spanish Conquistadors to Hidden Gold, Local Archaeologist Untangles the Truth from Myths of the Marble Mountain Caves in the Sangre de Cristo Mountains," I debunked several myths about the caves.

CHAPTER 3

Colorado College and the Peace Corps

I completed three years at Colorado College, traveling with two friends, Jim Cotton and Tricia Sohl, to Mexico after my studies. We took an eleven-day trip to Mexico. The Colorado College newspaper, *The Catalyst*, wrote an article about our adventures titled "Colorado College Students Splurge, Spent $60 on 11-Day Trip to Mexico." The newspaper wrote:

Wanta bet three Colorado College students can't make an 11-day trip into Mexico for $60?. . .

Armed with bed rolls, ponchos, the minimum of cloths and with Jim and Gary carrying ice axes (to be used as weapons against snakes), they drove to El Paso June 3 in Jim's car; parked it at a friend's house and walked to the international bridge.

There they ran into their first snag.

Mexican officials didn't think very highly of broke—so broke they had to hitch-hike—tourists. So, to get into

Mexico, the trio had to buy second-class train tickets to Chichuahua, 200 miles away.

Actually, they enjoyed the trip. Spending the money just meant that much less for food. (They all lost weight: Jim, nearly 10 pounds). . . .

Casualties: lost one can opener, had to depend on simpatico senoras to open can goods. Tricia lost pair of sneakers on beach at Acapulco and had to make return

Colorado College Students Splurge, Spend $60 On 11-Day Trip To Mexico

By MADELAINE WILSON

Wanta bet three Colorado College students can't make an 11-day trip into Mexico for $60?

A lively trio named Jim and Tricia and Gary believed they could, and did.

Home Thursday afternoon from their exciting adventures were Jim Cotton, 22, son of Mr. and Mrs. James Cotton, 742 E. Las Animas, who will be a senior next year majoring in political science and philosophy; Tricia Sohl, 20, daughter of Mr. and Mrs. Arthur H. Sohl, Wilton, Conn., who will be a junior majoring in history, and Gary Ziegler, 21, son of Mr. and Mrs. Raymond F. Ziegler, 509 N. Spruce, a senior majoring in philosophy and history.

What do these three have in common? Each is an only child. Each had a desire to meet Mexicans in their native habitat and each, perforce, had to make the trip economically.

Long-time friends, the three plotted their trip at "The Hub," student cafeteria, and it was to "The Hub" they returned this week for a rewarding treat — a long, tall glass of cold water without the addition of purifying tablets.

Gary is given credit for being the first to suggest the hitch-hiking trip in Mexico. But no arms were twisted to line up the other two.

Armed with bed rolls, ponchos, the minimum of clothes and with Jim and Gary carrying ice axes (to be used as weapons against snakes), they drove to El Paso June 3 in Jim's car, parked it at a friend's house and walked to the International bridge.

There they ran into their first snag.

Mexican officials didn't think very highly of broke—so broke they had to hitch-hike—tourists, so, to get into Mexico, the trio had to buy second-class train tickets to Chihuahua, 200 miles away.

Actually, they enjoyed the trip. Spending the money just meant that much less for food. (They all lost weight; Jim, nearly 10 pounds).

* * *

They paid for two sit-down meals during the trip — one in Mexico City, where they paid their only money for a hotel room — and one in Acapulco.

Most of their rides were in back ends of trucks under the broiling Mexican sun. One lucky break gave them nearly 800 miles in a car with a California couple who appreciated help with the driving. One bus ride was given free, courtesy the friendly driver. Another bus ride was paid for by a Mexican law student they met at a wayside stop when they were headed back to Mexico City from Acapulco.

Casualties: lost one can opener, had to depend on simpatico senoras to open can goods. Tricia lost pair of sneakers on beach at Acapulco and had to make return trip barefooted.

The time they were most afraid: during ride they accepted a truck. The driver invited them to his home, which proved to be some 20 miles off the main highway, and on a long bumpy, mountain road in an isolated area. However, the thatched roof house was beside a lake where they enjoyed swimming, and the hospitality was genuine. Next day, the driver took them back to their highway route.

Their trip's end conclusion: Have faith in the friendliness of people.

Now the trio is parted.

Tricia left by plane Friday for her home in Connecticut. She may transfer to another college this fall.

Gary will leave Sunday for Washington, D. C., and thence to Puerto Rico where he will instruct Peace Corps members in rock climbing technique. He is a member of the Mountain Climbing Club.

Jim leaves early in August for London where he will attend a three-week seminar on international relations at Studley College, sponsored by the American Friends Service Committee.

Jim Cotton, left; Tricia Sohl and Gary Ziegler, three Colorado College students who tested friendship in Mexico and found it fulfilling.

Article from the Colorado College newspaper,
The Catalyst, **date unknown**

trip barefooted. . . .

Now the trio is parted. . . .

Gary will leave Sunday for Washington, D.C., and thence to Puerto Rico where he will instruct Peace Corps members in rock climbing technique.

I had gotten the opportunity to teach rock climbing to Peace Corp volunteers and was excited to begin this new adventure. During the early 1960s, the Kennedy administration was putting the Peace Corps project together. One of the plans was to set up a training and evaluation camp for volunteers in the mountains of Puerto Rico. Thanks to Robert Ormes and his American Alpine Club connections, I flew to Washington, DC, for a job interview. I was hired to help set up a climbing challenge and jungle survival situation at the new camp during the summer of 1962.

Gary in the Peace Corps' Camp Radley, Puerto Rico, 1962

Dropping out of college for a year, I accumulated a number of interesting experiences. I worked briefly in the Peace Corps' Connecticut Avenue office in Washington, DC. I like to say that my main responsibility there was emptying the wastebaskets of administrators Daniel Patrick Moynihan and Bill Moyers while absorbing the positive political philosophy of the times.

America was on a roll with a "We can do it—let's make the world a better place and ask what you can do for your country" attitude. Arriving in Puerto Rico, I worked with a number of Peace Corps groups training for South American assignments.

While there, I was the guide for visiting Vice President Lyndon Johnson and Senator Maragret Chase Smith, a heady experience for a young Colorado boy. As it turned out, this work was connected with the first Outward Bound program in the United States.

Utilizing down time between programs, I hired on as crew for a sailing schooner out of nearby St. Thomas, learning sailing skills that launched a lifetime of sailing adventures. Then, best of all, I was assigned to visit Peace Corps groups I had worked with in Colombia and Ecuador. After touring much of the northern Andes in an embassy-loaned jeep and dispatching field reports, I returned home to Colorado, eager to resume my studies.

Two more academic years quickly passed. I guided climbing in the Tetons one summer. During another, I returned to Ecuador to climb 6,300-meter Chimborazo with Peace Corps friends.

Those were exciting times. We had just escaped nuclear holocaust with the Cuban Missile Crisis and President Kennedy was assassinated by a madman or, as some speculated, by a dark conspiratorial group.

I returned to Colorado College on an army scholarship, having previously completed the compulsory two years of Army ROTC at the school. Then I signed on for an additional two years. Looking back, it was excellent training, perhaps not West Point level but with solid courses in military history, tactics, field training, and leadership. We trained weekends down range at Fort Carson and attended a memorable summer camp, learning artillery basics and small-unit tactics at Fort Sill, Oklahoma. I still remember that experience in those dry, red sandstone hills. A classic artillery command to destroy a target, "Raise two and fire for effect," was yelled as dust covered us all and the 105 mm howitzer barked out a round.

Meanwhile, Colorado College academics got a bit messy. I had four years of intense geology study under noted Colorado geologist and author, Richard Pearl. With physics and solid science courses under my belt, I was surprised when I

Gary with friend Anne Forrest Ketchin at Colorado College, circa 1970

was told I would need to take organic chemistry to complete a geology degree.

At the time, I had been enthusiastically taking philosophy courses, following a passion for learning the history and intricacies of human thought, logic, and reason. A consultation with the department chairman, J. Glenn Gray, established that I would be able to graduate with a degree in philosophy without taking the dreaded chemistry course. Glenn Gray became my faculty adviser and, as it turned out, friend and mentor.

> J. Glenn Gray was a modern existential thinker, translator of philosopher Martin Heidegger, and World War II veteran. As an army combat intelligence officer, he had interviewed captive German generals at the Nuremberg Trials.
>
> His personal philosophy was to "calmly accept life as it comes." One of his books, *The Warriors: Reflections on Men in Battle*, became a guide, foundation, and focus for my own later Vietnam War and life experience.

Finally, the long-awaited event arrived. I graduated proudly with the coveted degree in hand and a commission as a second lieutenant in the US Army Reserve.

As the years moved by, my folks, Ray and Vi, built their small mining company into a successful operation. They teamed up with Colorado Springs-based Clarence Coil, a professional photographer and one of the founders of the Pikes Peak Range Riders. They continued to acquire and work mineral-rich mining properties while building an exceptional personal collection of Colorado crystals and minerals. Their company supplied specimens to collectors and museums around the world.

Ray and Vi Ziegler in Colorado Springs, circa 1962. Below: samples from their Colorado crystals and mineral collection. Left to right: agate-forming petrified wood; smoky quartz; and crystalline selenite, a type of gypsum.

CHAPTER 4

On the Road Again—Challenge, Adventure, and Chasing Desperados

In the spring of 1964, Stanley Shepard, a well-known climber from Boulder; a small group of other Colorado climbers; and I planned a climb and filming of an unclimbed ice peak in Peru's northern Andes. We were experienced mountaineers looking for a challenge. Having worked for the Peace Corps and climbed in South America, I ended up as the project leader. Our goal was to climb the nineteen-thousand-foot Nevado Cajavilca, which would be a much coveted first ascent in the Cordillera Blanca.

The expedition was sponsored by the American Alpine Club, supported by Colorado College Professor Bob Ormes, and *American Alpine Journal* editor Ad Carter. We were generously funded by local AAC member, Betsy Partridge, wife of NORAD commander General Earl Partridge. Our equipment was furnished by Holubar Mountaineering in

My climb up Nevado Cajavilca in August 1964
Courtesy of the Stanley Shepard Collection

Boulder. A portable Bolex 16 mm camera, state of the art at that time, and film were provided by the Alexander Film Company of Colorado Springs.

In Peru, Stan and I hired a porter with a mule to haul our camp and climbing gear to a base camp, miles up a very long canyon, Quebrada. The porter departed, leaving us minimally provisioned but eager for the climb. Nevado Cajavilca is attached by a long ridge to the twenty-thousand-foot peak,

Nevado Contrahiebas, which had previously been climbed. We needed to climb the ridge and then climb a high, steep, ice face culminating in the unclimbed summit. We placed a high camp at seventeen thousand feet, but at that point the weather became horrendously bad, with wind, blowing snow, and poor visibility. Against terrible odds, Stan and I struggled up and onto the summit.

Amid relief, joy and congratulations, the clouds briefly parted, giving a quick but revealing view of where we were.

**Gary climbing Nevado Atlante in
Peru's Cordillera Blanca**

Unbelievable! We were standing on top of the other peak—the one that had been climbed several times before. We had taken a wrong turn in the blinding clouds and failed in our attempt.

Retreating from the summit, Stan fell upside down into a deep crevasse. Evaluating the situation, I fixed the attached belay line to a quick snow picket and then captured the event with the Bolex. In preparation for such occurrences, we carried a handy set of nylon slings to use as prussic knot climbers, with which we could climb up a fixed line. Utilizing this tool, Stan was soon upright and beside me on solid glacier, shaken but okay.

The storm and snow continued for days. We were trapped in our tent at seventeen thousand feet, scarfing up the last several cans of tuna and chocolate bars. Fortunately, the small gas camp stove continued to melt snow, so we at least stayed reasonably hydrated. We occupied the time digging out the tent, which would have soon been buried in the heavy snowfall. Finally, in desperation, we began the dreaded descent down ice overhangs and steep ice slopes to our previous camp in the *quebrada* below. Leaving snow pickets and anchors behind, we accomplished the needed rappels and belayed descents to arrive below the snow line in one long day.

The next morning broke surprisingly clear and sunny. Stan managed a couple of cups of instant coffee to get us up and on the trail. We refused to leave behind the valuable remaining camp and climbing gear, so with heavy packs and empty stomachs, we staggered down the long trail back to the distant road and village. The topo map we carried indicated the distance to be some twenty miles. At least it was mostly downhill!

Moving slowly, utilizing the infamous mountain rest

step—step, rest-breath, step, repeat—we managed at most a couple of hundred yards and then had to sit down for several minutes to recover. What saved the day getting us out were doses of Dexedrine, a stimulant I kept in my emergency kit for just such a situation.

A day later we finally made the Andean Road to Huaraz. We found an upstairs room at a small road stop store and eatery there. With ravaging intensity, we immediately devoured plates of *pollo planchado*—fried chicken steak and potatoes. You might guess what happened next. We could keep nothing down and both immediately threw up the meal.

What finally brought us back to some degree of recovery and energy were frequent bowls of chopped bananas topped with sugar and Peru's famous canned milk, Leche Gloria. I have since joked about *mi amor Gloria* (my love Gloria.) As it turned out I shed some thirty pounds, which I never regained.

Perhaps calling the expedition a failure is not quite correct. Surviving the events, we experienced a fantastic life-challenging adventure that helped formulate my early "living life on the edge" philosophical approach to living well. This 1964 journey launched lifelong careers for both Stan and I in South America.

After this climb, I stayed to complete archaeological graduate studies at Peru's National University, San Marcos. At the time, San Marcos was a world center for international Andean studies. I had the good fortune of working with and studying under Edward Lanning, Jorge Muelle, Luis Lumbreras, and other notables of the time. We were involved with digs at Pacacamac, the Lurin Valley, Ancon, and associated Inca period Chancay sites. It was a great learning experience.

My interest in challenging adventures continued. This resulted in a focus on finding and documenting high Andean sites, perhaps a forerunner to what we now call "extreme archaeology." This is best exemplified by mountaineer-archaeologist Johan Reinhard and his remarkable discoveries of mummies on high ice peaks.

In 1965, my first cloud forest experience involved joining an expedition of armed Guardia Civil trekking to Vilcabamba's Espiritu Pampa, now known as the last refuge of the Inca. Our mission was to arrest American explorer, Gene Savoy, who reportedly was looting while encamped there.

I described this expedition in my book, *Machu Picchu's Sacred Sisters: Choquequirao & Llactapata*:

Savoy was a legendary explorer and eccentric self-promoter, founder of his own Reno, Nevada, church and authentic discoverer of the real "Lost City of the Incas" — Vilcabamba at Espiritu Pampa. He had a sort of cult following of attractive and wealthy women. His modus

Journalist Jorge Moreau and police on the trail to Espiritu Pampa, 1965

operandi was to find a site, or several loosely associated groups, then claim it was part of a huge complex encompassing many square miles. If something later was found by someone else, it was only a part of his Grand something or other.

While I was studying at San Marcos, the national university in Lima, the news was full of Savoy's discoveries at Espiritu Pampa. Sponsored by the Patronata de Arqueologia, predecessor to the INC (Instituto Nacional de Cultura) and the newspaper, *El Comercio*, Jorge Moreau, journalist and head photographer from the paper and I organized a group to check out his reports.[3] Some suspected that he was looting the site, so our job was to gather the truth. As these were the years of the violent Hugo Blanco insurgency, we traveled well-armed, with a contingent of national police and army mules. Struggling through deep mud and pouring rains of the rainy season in January 1965, we arrived to verify Savoy's work as legitimate. Many years later, I conveyed this story to Savoy, who humorously told me that he was hiding at the village of Lucma, watching us with binoculars as we rode

---

[3] Jorge Moreau, his wife Silvia, and I became close friends while I lived and studied in Lima. They rented a comfortable room to me in a fancy apartment they owned in Lima's upscale Miraflores district. We also shared a photo lab that Jorge had nearby. We lost contact when I left for home, Colorado, and Army duty. Then—out of the blue—I received a courteous email while writing this chapter in December 2025. "Gary—it's Jorge, I'm still alive—please reply." And so I did. Wow—who would believe this? They are now US citizens living in Florida. He is 86, she 83. They led extensive interesting, sometimes dangerous, lives since last we talked almost sixty years ago. Jorge, born in Argentina was arrested, beaten, and imprisoned during the violent military coup days there in the 1970s. His stories and adventures go on and on.

past, wondering who the pistol-toting Gringo was. He expected to be arrested if found, which of course he would have been.

During this time, I even tried my hand at filming Machu Picchu, but that career failed. Despite this, my degree and experiences firmly launched my interest in Vilcabamba and the 1537 -1572, Neo- Inca colonial era.

Uncle Sam requested that I drop out for a few years to complete my Colorado College army ROTC Army commitment. So, putting my doctorate on hold, I left Peru and headed off to the army.

**Gary tried his hand at filming at Machu Picchu in 1965
using the portable Bolex 16 mm camera he bought,
but that was a career that failed.**

CHAPTER 5

Dodging Proverbial Bullets and the Second-Best View in the Country

Sometime in the late 1960s, while awaiting a pending active duty army assignment, I used the opportunity to visit the Tetons. I had climbed some of the major routes and peaks there when I worked briefly one summer for Glen Exum's mountain guide service.

Loading climbing and camping gear in a battered old Volkswagen, I set out northward accompanied by a gal I was dating at the time named Leonor. We had climbed together around the Pikes Peak area, the Garden of the Gods, and North Cheyenne, so I knew she was very capable.

I don't remember much about the long drive across Wyoming except for one memorable morning. Driving past Dubois, the first rays of dawn brilliantly illuminated the spectacular, jagged, glacier-topped peaks of the Teton range in all their geomorphic magnificence. My thought was that this had to be the best mountain view in the country. A few years later, I discovered a similar well-kept secret in Custer

**Gary and his dog Neal climbing in the
Garden of the Gods circa 1970**

County, our special mountain view of the Sangre de Cristos, what the Ute once called "the Shining Mountains."

We arrived at my old guiding hangout, Moose, Wyoming. After signing in at Park Headquarters, we moved on to camp at one of the designated areas. After a couple of days hiking and a trip into Jackson Hole, we decided on a climb of the Middle Teton's Black Dike Route. I suspect the choice of this peak was influenced by remembering that Colorado's great pioneer mountaineer Albert Ellingwood, also a graduate of

Colorado Springs High School and Colorado College, had made the first ascent climb in 1923.

I had climbed the Black Dike route once before. It was challenging, but not too difficult. I thought we would be able to summit, enjoy an easy down climb, and then take a leisurely hike back to camp. We loaded essential emergency gear into our climbing packs, including down jackets, wool hats, gloves, headlamps, a basic first aid kit, a waterproof bivouac sack, and an insulating pad.

This was basic emergency preparation, which I had taught, along with survival and climbing, for the Peace Corps and early Outward Bound programs. However, being a hot-shot young climber, I foresaw no problems and assumed we

wouldn't need the equipment.

Having signed in the climb plan to authorities the night before, we headed out and up to the base of the East Face early on that fateful day. Along with our packs, we carried a treasured, new 150-foot coil of Perlon continuous-core climbing rope. My sling-loaded protection rack had an assortment of Chouinard-Frost chrome-moly pitons. I also had a few of the chocks that could be wedged into cracks as removable, reusable anchors. Some of the climbing hardware was my own design, made in a basement shop setup at my folk's place in Colorado Springs.

As will be described later, in 1971, I teamed up with the Lowe brothers, Mike, Greg, and Jeff, and bought Bear Basin Ranch, located around ten miles east of Westcliffe. Renting a shop in town, Mike started making prototype climbing equipment. The business became Lowe Alpine Systems, a successful and well-known outdoor recreational equipment manufacturer based near Boulder.

But that is a story for a later chapter. Today I was in the Tetons, hiking until we reached the base of a cliff with a prominent vertical dipping basaltic dike—the namesake feature of the climb. Belaying each other, we made good time up the lower wall.

After these many years, I don't remember the exact route, but I recall occasionally traversing back and forth across the dike. It was on one of these crossovers that tragedy struck! I was up some seventy-five feet above Leonor, overconfidently leading without clipping into an in-place piton or placing protection. There was nothing between us but rope. I came to a thick column of ice, which filled the crevice I needed to cross. I stepped on top of it, reaching for a handhold on the other side.

CRACK! The ice broke loose!

Airborne, I shot past Leonor in full free fall. Then unbelievably, I was yanked to a stop some seventy-five feet below her. Miraculously, she had caught me. Her anchor held and the stretch of the rope absorbed much of the force, allowing her body-belay to hold against all odds on such a long fall.

Then—another surprise. The rope retracing from the high-force stretch, pulled violently upward, slamming me against an overhanging projection above. What saved me from serious injury was a good helmet and the backpack taking most of the impact. Unfortunately, I did smash an elbow into the rock, which resulted in a painful fracture and partial immobility of my right arm.

Whew—now what? I was hanging free under an overhang some seventy-five feet below my belayer, still a bit stunned that I was alive.

Fortunately, training and preparation saved the day. Reaching into a parka pocket, I pulled out three loops of thin nylon carried for just such a situation. With one and a half functioning hands, I attached the nylon to the taut climbing rope with prussic knots, followed by long slings to serve as stirrups. The small loops, when wrapped several times around the climbing rope, can be slid upward and will hold in place when weight is placed on them.

Using a sort of one-two-three technique—weight on two, slide up one—it was possible to climb steadily, slowly upward. This system was used before mechanical ascenders called Jumars were developed.

After what seemed an agonizing eternity, I pulled myself up onto the ledge beside Leonor. She was terrified, frozen painfully in place, unable to release or free herself from the tightened rope. She had saved us from certain death. This fit, 110-pound girl had caught and held me after I fell around one hundred-fifty feet. It was unbelievable!

Untangling from ropes and gear, we realized that I could not climb on. It was now late enough that attempting a rope rappel down was not practical. We would have to overnight on the small belay ledge. I knew that a rescue team would be sent out tomorrow when we did not check in. Putting pride aside, in the worst-case scenario, we could wait for that.

Thus began the night from hell!

Gary and Leonor

It began to rain, switching to wind-propelled, swirling hail. At least we would not suffer from dehydration. Our emergency gear saved our butts. We donned the extra jackets underneath now leaking rain parkas, spreading out the foam insulating pad to sit on. The pièce de résistance was huddling together under the bivouac sack. As the tumultuous night progressed, I gobbled whatever pain pills we had in the first aid kit, which somewhat subdued the elbow pain.

Finally, the storm broke clear as the first rays of sun seeped over the eastern horizon. After singing snippets of the Beatles lyrics from their song, "Here Comes the Sun," we prepared for the long, difficult descent. Shortening the story, we reached the glacier below just as the rescue team arrived. The drive back to Colorado was uneventful. Leonor completed her classes at Colorado College while I prepared to head to Georgia for mandated army duty.

Off on separate paths, a continent apart, my life-saving friend Leonor and I parted for different commitments and projects after our harrowing adventure. I owed her big time. As fate would have it, the opportunity came along for repayment.

I was stationed in Georgia, absorbing training with an assortment of interesting assignments and jobs that the army then provided to career-focused young officers. I learned small-unit tactics and command protocol for infantry, armor, field intelligence, long-range patrols, and more. I was even allowed to play polo on occasion.

I briefly was assigned as a training company commander and several times escorted prisoners to federal facilities in New York. I also gathered a few flying lessons, which would prove useful during my later combat tour in Vietnam.

Leonor was pursuing professional dance training in New York City while attending Saint Lawrence University. We got together briefly during my prisoner escort duty.

At the end of one summer, I had leave available. Leonor invited me to visit and meet her family in Ohio. We would then drive on to New York City together for her return to fall classes. It was a fun and interesting visit. She came from an active, intellectual, well-educated family. I remember talking at length about Thor Heyerdahl's voyage of the *Kon Tiki* and its anthropological significance with her dad. The family generously gifted me a classic 1930s mandolin, which I still have today.

We left for New York City and after a long day's drive, we found ourselves somewhere near the Pine Barrens in New Jersey. I believe we stopped in Lebanon State Park. We planned to overnight there and drive on to New York City the following day.

The park was pretty much deserted, so we drove until we found an empty parking area surrounded by brush and tall pines. This would do nicely. It was a warm night, just getting dark. After traveling overland around South America and Mexico, I had a good awareness of safety. We decided to camp some distance out in the pines, away from the vehicle. If anyone drove in, we would hear them but would not be seen.

Picking a flat spot a couple of hundred feet away, we spread out sleeping pads and blankets. Unknown to Leonor, I had a loaded pistol that I always kept handy when traveling. I quietly laid it out next to me along with our flashlight. I had extensive experience with firearms from my time in Peru and army training.

Just after dark, we were lying comfortably with big pillows on the pads, blankets spread over us. Having not seen anyone drive in, we were casually talking, planning out tomorrow's events.

Suddenly, a branch snapped very close.

I instinctually rolled off the pad, grabbing the pistol and flashlight! THUNK!! A heavy object crashed down where I had just been lying, fortunately missing Leonor. With an airborne tuck and roll, I came upright with the flashlight on and a cocked pistol.

G Ziegler in Georgia with a new Ducati

Standing there was a massive, ugly character in a black leather jacket, holding what appeared to be a raised baseball bat. I growled threateningly, blinding him with the light. "Move and you are dead," I said.

He had likely heard the distinctive click of the pistol cocking. I was now in full combat mode, coming close to pulling the trigger. Fortunately, he lowered the club and stepped back. Strangely, he seemed shocked that I had a gun.

Whew—what to do now?

I was standing in my underwear, and I was barefoot. I decided to march him out to the parking lot away from Leonor. We left her, and he kept his hands raised as I followed him. Reaching the road, he broke into a run.

With relief I let him go, making sure he left. I returned to the frightened Leonor. We hurriedly gathered our belongings and returned to our car. We drove on through the night to the big city in silence. I caught a flight back to Georgia from La Guardia the next afternoon.

It had indeed been an interesting vacation.[4]

---

[4] What I had not known about Leonor was that she had become a practicing Quaker, dedicated to pacifism and avoidance of violence. We lost contact then. I hope all has gone well for her over the years. I remember her as a treasured and very talented friend.

CHAPTER 6

The Army and Vietnam Remembered: How We Almost Won the War

As fate and luck would have it, I was assigned to several unique units, first at Nha Trang in August 1966, and then with 1st MIBARS ARS (Military Intelligence Battalion Aerial Exploitation Aerial Reconnaissance Support), nicknamed the Flying Eye Battalion. I was attached to its Headquarters Command (HHC) from January through July of 1967.

The assignment gave me a rare opportunity to utilize my

My unit badge and Special Forces Membership card

We didn't get this one home, but the crew miraculously survived.

skills and an unusual level of personal freedom to shape operations normally reserved for more senior officers. Later, with MACV (Military Assistance Command Vietnam) and J-2 (intelligence) field operations, I saw much of the country and served with several exceptional units and men.

I soon became involved with aerial recon development and other active intel activities. I called on the training and experiences I had had in South America with the Peace Corps and my archaeology graduate studies in Peru.

The CIA had tried to hire me, but the army had first rights and my allegiance.

We began flying photo recon FAC (Forward Air Control) missions from Nha Trang in support of the Fifth Special Forces Group and others shortly after I arrived. It turned out that flying low over hostiles at less than one hundred miles per hour was problematic. Luckily, most of the time we didn't take fire, as smarter adversaries knew that a sortie of ordinance-laden A-1Es or F-4s soon followed when they gave away their position.

We received basic touch-and-go flight training to help the pilot's workload and take over when the worst happened. I probably could have brought one of our "Good Guy" U-6s home and on the ground intact if needed. The higher-ups had doubts we could handle a Huey, so it was "just grab the collector and hope for the best." Being Signal Corps trained, I could at least handle the radios.

After moving to MIBARS headquarters in Saigon, I was attached to MACV J-2, becoming field operations assistant to USAF lieutenant colonel Harry Holeman, a charismatic World War II ace fighter pilot and physicist. His cover story was that he ran a photo lab and was a MACV science adviser.

Yeah, right!

I remember him in a quiet huddle with Robert McNamara, the US secretary of defense, and Ellsworth Bunker, who afterwards was awarded the Presidential Medal of Freedom.

But, Harry did take photos.

Harry Holeman's cover story was that he ran a photo lab and was MACV science adviser.

Lieutenant Ziegler and Major Jack Fletcher with an Australian Army Cessna 180 D, FAC

We used to say we were "just surveying enemy fire accuracy for President Johnson." Humor and levity were our saviors and sanity in those dangerous days. Harry pulled me out of army obscurity and made me his assistant. Perhaps he recognized that we had some similar talents and philosophy, but he gave me his trust and allowed me to put together a handpicked field team for deploying all sorts of classified

---

Harry's Mission Statement

Visit every major ground unit in the country. Go to Special Forces camps, ground reconnaissance units, armored cavalry units, and water-borne reconnaissance units. Search everywhere for intelligence sources—long-range patrols, boats, electronic surveillance, and agent operations. Don't get bogged down by dog-and-pony shows staged for colonels and generals. When I want special info, go get it and get back with it. Be prepared to brief me or the general as soon as you return.

Gary at his desk in *Tan Son Nhut*

items against Charlie (the Viet Cong).

We collected intelligence and related project information as a direct, inside source. We were involved in most of what was going on operationally around the country, including recon patrols, FAC flights, and the use and placement of high-tech sensors. I was attached for some time to the US Fifth Special Forces Group and accompanied Australian major Jack Fletcher on various SAS (Special Air Service) missions. Despite our difference in rank, we became close friends.

Fred Edwards was also active with the US Secretive Special Operations Group (SOG) and kept us in that loop. We hitched rides on Air America flights, ARVIN C7s, Caribous, and everything else.[5] As you can guess, we carried top, broad, need-to-know security clearances. It was indeed a challenging and exciting time. Orders signed by the J-2 got us almost everywhere with no questions asked.

Meanwhile, I kept a desk at Tan Son Nhut Air Base and a bunk at the nearby MIBARS compound, thanks to then MIBARS commander, Gene Kelly. A most stressful moment as a young lieutenant during downtime in Saigon was giving a formal briefing to General William Westmoreland and his staff. Later I occasionally briefed M. G. McChristian, who was not quite as intimidating.

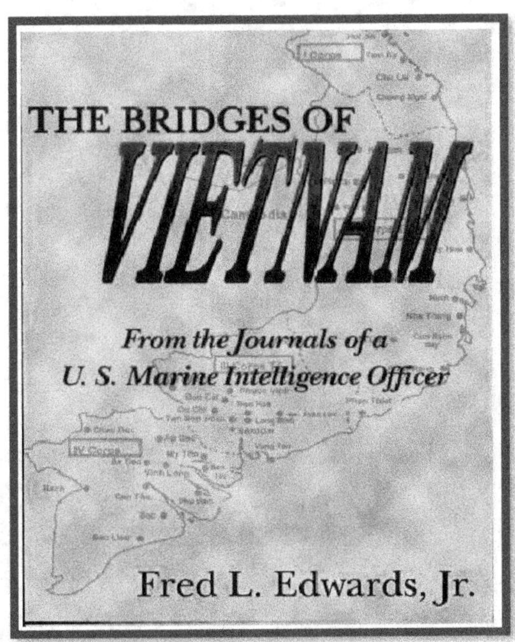

---

[5] Fred Edwards was a US marine major attached to MACV J-2 (intelligence). Harry Holeman and his boss M. G. McChristan assigned Fred to our small "does not exist" team. We worked together with Australian army major Jack Fletcher. Fred later punished his journals in which we all appear. We reconnected in the late 1990s by email, shortly before he died.

For the remainder of 1967, my team of several senior NCOs and I bounced all over while based in Saigon. I was TDY (temporary duty) to the Australian SAS (Special Air Service) unit near Vung Tau with the aforementioned SAS major Jack Fletcher.

Jack Fletcher and Gary somewhere in Vietnam, 1967

> ### The Rock Pile
>
> (From *Time*, October 7, 1966)
>
> *"The terrain was as tough as any the U.S. Marines had ever contested. It combined the horror of a Guadalcanal jungle with the exhausting steepness of the slopes at Chapultepec. Added to that were fusillades of bullets as ferocious as at Tarawa and showers of shrapnel that turned the forest into a tropical Belleau Wood. "The Rock Pile""as Viet Nam's latest big battleground has come to be called. . . .*
>
> *Key to the fighting is "the Rock," a jagged, 750-ft. fang of granite that thrusts upward at the intersection of three river valleys and two enemy trails. During July's Operation Hastings, the Marines established a reconnaissance post atop the Rock, and a lone sniper fed by airdrops of C rations controlled the area. Now it is a Marine battalion command post, under almost steady siege."*

Sometime in 1967, my team and I helicoptered onto The Rock Pile for an eventful stay with a small US Marine Corps detachment, who were "holding down the fort" if you will. A small contingent operated at the summit with sophisticated detection and communication equipment that was thought critical to the entire intelligence operation in South Vietnam.

Aside from visual observation, their exact purpose was top secret. Our mission was to evaluate efficiency and needs there. We also upgraded several of the sensors. Otherwise, the view toward the mountainous DMZ (demilitarized zone) was a threat. That being said, we were most happy to leave it to the US Marines as we enjoyed the several flights back to Saigon. We returned to Da Nang in a vibrating, ancient Sikorsky H-34 marine helicopter and then traveled onward in a modern US Air Force C-130.

Sometime in 1967, Colonel Holeman and I flew to Tokyo

They even gave Gary an award for the work he did

to secretly purchase hi-tech intel items. Of course, he spoke Japanese. With our orders signed by M. G. McChristian, nobody questioned who we were or what we did. We bunked at the US leased, downtown Tokyo Hotel Sanno, in the bachelor officers' quarters; attended a Buck Owens concert; and shamelessly ate gourmet Kobe beef dinners supplied by our unofficial Japanese Defense Force hosts. After a duty like this, I passed up an authorized rest and recreation vacation opportunity.

It was indeed a strange war.

Back in Saigon, we dined on Chinese food and watched "Puff the Magic Dragon" AC-47s light up the near horizon during happy hour at the downtown Caravelle Hotel rooftop bar.

Should we have been in Vietnam? Probably not.

At the time, that was not our concern. The bad guys we dispatched were truly deserving. To hell with geo-politics, there was a coordinated plan of Maoist revolutionary terrorism in place to kill or terrorize all who might object to Ho Chi Min's takeover plans.

We vividly experienced this policy firsthand. (Later I saw the same Maoist-style atrocities executed in the Andes of Peru by the insurgent Sendero Luminoso group during the 1980s.) The South had its share of warlords and corruption, but nothing to equal the atrocity, terror, and death brought on deliberately by the invading North.

On occasion, I give my own analysis of how we became involved in Vietnam, step-by-step, following World War II. Looking back at that history, I can see how it almost logically happened. Probably the best explanation is given by historian, Barbara Tuchman in her 1985 book *The March of Folly: From Troy to Vietnam*. It is not favorable to US policy but makes it understandable. I also recommend Bernard Fall's book, *Street Without Joy*, for background on the defeat of the French, the founding of the Viet Cong, and the long-planned invasion of South Vietnam.

Upon returning home, I started Bear Basin Ranch near

Westcliffe, Colorado, lectured part-time at Colorado College, and ran anthropological education courses in Mexico's Sierra Madre for Outward Bound and Colorado College.[6]

---

[6] Major General Bentley Rayburn (USAF RET), a good friend and fellow member of our Pikes Peak Range Riders group, encouraged the writing of this chapter, suggesting many helpful additions and changes.

Colonel Ted Severn (USA RET), also a Range Rider and close friend, helped with thoughtful suggestions and encouragement. We have shared endless stories of our service in Vietnam as young lieutenants and have also sailed the Caribbean together.

A special thanks goes to another encouraging old friend, Joe Barrera. We have travelled the wilds of Pancho Villa's Sierra Madre together on foot and horseback, rode hard and worked cattle on the ranch, and shared numerous adventures. Joe, a Colorado College graduate and PhD professor was, as he terms it, a "lead the patrol grunt" during the vicious engagements in the Central Highlands with the Fourth Infantry Division.

CHAPTER 7

Bear Basin Ranch in Custer County

Fresh out of graduate school, the army, and a combat tour in Vietnam, I was managing Spencer Penrose's old ranch, Emerald Valley, above the Broadmoor in Colorado Springs. Looking for calmer places and a new direction. I saw an ad for a place for sale near Westcliffe, Colorado which looked appealing. It turned out to be 350 acres and a group of run-down, abandoned buildings that had been built around 1890, located in the heart of the Wet Mountains. The price was right: $80 per acre with a low down payment. I bought it immediately. This began the story of modern Bear Basin Ranch.[7]

---

[7] At the time, I was living and working with Anne Forrest Ketchin. We had met during my time in Georgia. We bought the ranch together, but she moved on to complete a doctorate at Colorado University, becoming a famous Southwest anthropologist.

Bear Basin Ranch with the Sangre de Cristo Range in the background

Bear Basin Ranch, circa 1970

The land on which Bear Basin Ranch now sits was originally prime hunting ground for roaming bands of buffalo hunters and later one of the summer camping areas for the Mountain Utes. In the mid-1870s, the ranch was covered by miners looking to strike it rich in the mad rush to find silver and gold. Over the following years, the land served as a homestead and a cattle ranch.

The earlier residents had long abandoned the place. The Rosco family last lived there in the 1950s. It was now owned by Marvin Ham, who lived in Penrose. Marvin ran a few summer cows and shared grazing with resident neighbor Lee Jones.

After I shooed residing cows out of the houses, patched roofs, and replaced windows, the place was soon almost habitable. Bidding Emerald Valley goodbye, I moved in while continuing to run the occasional outdoor program for

Bear Basin Ranch, circa 1971

Outward Bound and my old alma mater, Colorado College, to keep a cash flow going.

I rounded up several friends to come in as investors. Our vision was to develop an outdoor educational facility while creating a working ranch and retreat well away from Richard Nixon's urban madness.

Mike Lowe and his brothers Jeff and Greg tossed in some bucks to get things rolling. Mike and his wife, Carol, moved into the bunkhouse. I claimed the Larey cabin. Carol secured a teaching position with Custer County School while Mike and I were off working winter Outward Bound programs on skis in the San Juans. Colorado College anthropology professor Mike Nowak also came in with us.

The Lowes went on to found Lowe Alpine Systems, a successful mountaineering equipment manufacturer, which they eventually sold for millions. We like to claim that it all started at the ranch.

Lee Jones and his wife, Anna

As surrounding land became available, we continued to buy and lease, eventually reaching the four thousand or so acres the ranch encompasses today. Meanwhile Lee Jones, our closest neighbor, and I became fast friends. I had horse packed in South America and briefly played polo in the army but had no real ranching experience. He was happy to take me on as his apprentice.

Gary learning to cut hay using a horse team, circa 1975

Combining our pastures, we ran a summer yearling cow operation while training and trading a growing remuda of horses, which eventually reached eighty head. He preferred Appaloosas so I soon had a registered Appaloosa stallion named Ben for breeding and riding. Ben sired a long line of excellent, colorful working horses, which we later used on the ranch and for pack trips in the nearby Sangre de Cristos.

Lee would take me to the livestock sales at Salida, Pueblo, and La Junta to buy and sell horses. We bid against southern Colorado horse trader notables like Tony Cucharas, Frank Zavislan, Jim Gerhart, and the Disanti brothers. I learned to watch the casual winks and cigar flicks to know who was bidding and who was abstaining.

We would bring the horses home to Bear Basin in my somewhat restored 1947 Diamond T stock truck and then sort them out in the big wood-rail corrals. I would ride the rough ones, Lee shouting encouragement when I frequently hit the ground. We would sell the good ones "guaranteed" to suitable buyers. The others went back to the "buyer beware" sale barns.

The ranch house which became my home after Lee's death

Eventually, Lee pretty much retired, leaving me to run both ranches. He kept a gentle horse or two for a ride on the ranch. We frequently went to Westcliffe together for lunch at Susie and Danny Loafman's popular cafe. Lee loved Susie's "Western Sandwich" with greasy fries on the side and bitter, day-old coffee. Sometimes Danny would be there with his guitar, belting out a Charlie Pride favorite like "Kiss an Angel Good Morning" while Barb Stock and Susie's sister Belinda cheerfully served up the meals.

Lee generously arranged his will so that I would be able to buy the Jones Ranch at a very low cost from his estate. This added another thousand aces including the old 1870s log house, which became my home and headquarters, often just referred to as the ranch house.

Gary in front of the bunkhouse, circa 1970

Rancher demands simple life of adventure

By Jeff Daly
Colorado Springs Sun

American author Henry David Thoreau believed the essential necessity of life was simplicity, and its standard of value measured in "vital experience."

Nearing 40 when he took refuge at Walden Pond, Thoreau concluded that dealing with the complexities of civilization relegated most people to lives "of quiet desperation."

While other middle-aged men look with chagrin at unfulfilled ambitions, Gary Ziegler knows no such dismay. He describes his experience as a life of fantasy, grounded in self-reliant simplicity.

Now 40, he owns a 3,000-acre ranch and 50 horses near Westcliff. Home is a three-room, turn-of-the-century log cabin lit with kerosene lamps and heated by a wood-burning stove.

Well water is pumped by hand and stored in cans. Rustic outhouses deteriorate along with other outbuildings near the ranch's barn. A 30-foot well serves as a refrigerator.

With no running water, there is no bath, but hot showers for two-bits are only 11 miles away in Silver Cliff.

"It's been a neat feeling to be out here for 11 years being self-sufficient," Ziegler said while sipping whiskey in the comfort of his cabin.

"Man needs constant challenges and must live on the naked edge of experience to lead a vital life," Ziegler said. "It's through the situations you place yourself in that you find the meaning of life."

His history reads like an adventure novel.

As a youth in Colorado Springs, he had conquered most of Colorado's 14,000-foot peaks by age 16.

He studied geology and philosophy at Colorado College, and his zeal for adventure led to a series of "vital experiences" from the Andes Mountains in South America to the humid jungles of Southeast Asia.

In his junior year of college, he was hired by the Peace Corps to train volunteers in survival skills in Puerto Rico. Later, he was chosen by the Peace Corps to travel throughout South America as a program evaluator.

"There were a lot of good people involved and the level of idealism was just incredible," Ziegler recalled.

Idealistic himself — a quality that permeates his perceptions today — and with a yen for knowledge, Ziegler returned to Colorado Springs to complete his philosophy studies.

When the ink on his diploma was barely dry, Ziegler organized an expedition and set out for Peru to film ascents of 20,000-foot peaks no one had climbed before. Later he would film such an ascent for National Geographic magazine.

That first perilous climb nearly cost him and a companion their lives.

"We were snowed in for six days above 18,000 feet with no food," he said.

The two eventually stumbled and crawled back to a mountain village where they were restored to health by local peasants.

Recovered, they hitch-hiked to the capital city of Lima, where Ziegler taught English at the University of San Marcos.

During the next two years he combined study with teaching and earned a master's degree in an-

See RANCHER, page 3

'Man needs constant challenges and must live on the naked edge of experience to lead a vital life.'
— Gary Ziegler

Photos by Pete Mugaas, special to The Sun

Gary Ziegler on his ranch near the Sangre de Cristo Mountains

Colorado Springs *Sun* article featuring Gary and describing his "simple life" at Bear Basin Ranch, date unknown

CHAPTER 8

Bear Basin Ranch's First Pack Trip

I realized early on that I would not be able to make land payments by just ranching. With my education, army training, and experience as a climbing guide, I thought it made sense to develop programs and activities along these lines that could supplement income from cattle and horses.

In 1972, an Outward Bound instructor friend Rick Medrick, Arlie Riggs, and I formed a rafting company on the Arkansas River using our whitewater experience running trips through the big Colorado River canyons. We named it simply Arkansas River Tours. The company lives on today, one of several dozen serving a booming tourist industry. I sold out my share to Rick in the early 1980s to concentrate on expanding activities at Bear Basin.

The Bear Basin-based guide and outfitting business also started around 1972. With support from local State Wildlife Officer Dan Riggs and his wife, Arlie, as well as ranching friends Floyd and Mary Kattnig and others, I soon had the

Celia Jensen and Lee Jones give advice as I hitch on the loads. "Hoping you do a better job than how you roofed your barn," said Lee.

needed US Forest Service permits to begin running multiple-day horse trips in the surrounding mountains, along with hunting and guided climbs of the Crestone Peaks.

Dan generously showed me the high valleys, old cow camps, and almost lost trails that would become so important to the growing pack trip business. I learned his secrets of where the big elk and bucks hung out and where alpine lake trout were big as submarines.

One of our first guided trips took place in the summer of 1972. I, with friends Celia Jensen and Judith Ames, left Bear

Basin Ranch on a multi-day adventure. We rode beside an almost deserted Highway 96 into Westcliffe and then up South Colony Road. I believe we camped at the Canda family sawmill on the way. Having graciously agreed to take on ranch chores while we were gone, Celia returned back to town and onward to the ranch.

Judith, the horses, and I continued up to South Colony Lake, where we made a high camp, picketing the horses out on a lush alpine meadow.[8] We both very much wanted to climb one or more of the Crestone mountains while there.

My memories are of a harrowing, difficult climb up the Ellingwood Route on Crestone Needle in dubious weather. Cold, tired, and discouraged, I nearly quit while leading the particularly challenging section just below the summit. As you may recall, I had originally climbed the same route at age

The location of Bear Basin Ranch and the ranch house along Colorado Highway 96

---

[8] Judith was a great granddaughter of Teddy Rosevelt. She went on to graduate from Harvard and became a noted designer for Koyori Furniture in Seattle.

Climbing up the Ellingwood Route on Crestone Needle

fourteen with legendary mountaineer Robert Ormes.

Judith supplied the spark that saved the moment by shouting up something like, "Come on mountain man, you can do it." We summited and then carefully picked our way back down the easier but longer descent route to the camp.

A day or two later, we rode back to Westcliffe, making town in one long day. WHEW! We overnighted with horses in the yard of a friend's house on Second Street after wolfing down a much enjoyed greasy fried chicken special at nearby Susie's Cafe. We might have even had a shot or two of her famous house hooch while her husband Danny Loafman belted out a slightly altered version of Willie Nelson's "Denver" lyrics on his old Martin D-18 guitar, substituting Westcliffe in for Denver in the song.

After multiple coffees the next morning, Lee Jones cheerfully arrived with a stock truck more battered than we were to haul us all home. Yeehaw!

Our pack trips continued, with the goal to keep the land and facilities as close as possible to a working, traditional, Old West ranch. We continued developing public horse programs and educational events on the ranch while carefully avoiding guest ranch activities. A wilderness tent camp, teepees, and a yurt were set up for overnight camping out of sight and away from roads. The old log structures at the headquarters served as summer staff lodging, a trip logistics center, and the main office. We also added the Bear Basin Environmental Resource Center School of Mountaineering, using my climbing and Outward Bound experience.

Annie Carter joins Gary on a climb up Lover's Leap on the Hardscrabble Pass in 1960

Real living
Is
Walking the edge.
A thin line
Further in than out
Closer to
Being.

BEAR BASIN ENVIRONMENTAL
RESOURCE CENTER
SCHOOL OF MOUNTAINEERING

CHAPTER 9

Law West of Pueblo and Why Jane Fonda Moved On

Pulling out an old sawed-off double 12-gauge shotgun, I stepped out. It was a classic "Treasure of the Sierra Madre" standoff. There were four of them, a tire iron, and knives. . . . Would I shoot? We stared each other down like Gary Cooper in High Noon.

It was hot during the dry summer of 1971. Law enforcement west of Pueblo in the small mountain town of Westcliffe, Colorado, was pure Old West, headed up by Sheriff Stan De-Priest, a weathered lawman straight out of a Louis L'Amour novel.

I had rolled into Colorado's sparely populated Custer County on an old BMW motorcycle, fresh from the morass of Vietnam and an abandoned army career that my maternal ancestors would have expected me to pursue. A philosophy degree from Colorado College and a graduate school education were influencing me to seek a calmer rural life. Working part-time for Colorado Outward Bound; running climbing, survival, and wilderness programs; shoeing horses; and riding out colts, I was slowly getting dilapidated Bear Basin Ranch, bought with all my savings and a big mortgage, back in operation.

It was, in a way, returning to origins. My dad, Ray Ziegler, a geologist and Colorado history buff, had frequently taken me poking around the old mining properties in the area as a child. As I got to know the county around Bear Basin Ranch, I got to know Sheriff Stan and learned he had ample backup: a ranch-raised wife, Ruby Vickerman; a capable full-time deputy, Norm Jordan, who was a retired army sargeant and weight lifter and tougher than a junk yard dog; and a couple of dedicated, six-gun-toting "special deputies" living around the county. These seasoned rural guys kept the lid on happenings in their respective areas. There was little need for trained rescue teams or sophisticated law enforcement in those simpler times.

Stan drove a big family sedan with a "gumball" light on top and with the one department radio—a long wave whip antenna device most likely left over from World War II—taking up most of the front seat. The radio could sometimes reach the State Patrol office in Canyon City or Pueblo. The rural deputies used their personal pickups with red lights and magnetic stick-on door signs proclaiming, "Sheriff Custer County."

Westcliffe, in proper western tradition, had a town marshal supplemented by Stan and Norm when the cowboys came to town Saturday nights for the dance at Susie's Cafe. Lead guitarist Danny Loafman, backed by the Wet Mountain Boys, served up a potpourri of country favorites lubricated by rounds of Jack Daniel's.

The courthouse had an old two-cell slammer. The lawmen would stick the rowdies in there overnight and then send them packing back to cattle ranges in the morning. Rarely was a charge filed or the County Judge needed. Ruby served them up a great breakfast.

Soon CB radios came along. Most everyone installed one of these squawking, annoying devices, which worked okay some of the time. They did, however, provide everyone in the county an opportunity to listen in, give advice, and get involved in sheriff affairs. There were few secrets in Custer County at that time.

Sometime about then, Jane Fonda, a friend of Susie and Danny, came to town to film *There Comes a Horseman*. Many of us worked on the set, located near Lake DeWeese, with the sheriff providing security. My 1947 Diamond T truck and horses starred in several scenes. County Commissioner George Draper supplied most of the livestock.

Jane briefly considered buying a place here but decided to move on. Remembered for her infamous visit to Hanoi during

Jane throws a neat loop but loses her hat.

Courtesy of John Bryson

the war by several folks, she was about as popular as sheep on a cattle pasture in some county circles.

Meanwhile, deputies came and went. Norm retired to Silver Cliff, replaced by former Steamboat Springs town patrolman Ken Perschbacher. Ken, a motivated, talented guy, would later become founder of Custer County's search and rescue unit along with local Division of Wildlife (DOW) officer Dan Riggs and me.

I was invited one weekend to a neighborhood party, to discuss local crime issues. Our part of Custer County, referred to by more affluent valley ranchers as "them poor East Hills," was being hit hard by rural burglaries, particularly in newly created subdivisions vogue at the time. Vacant dwellings with few full-time residents made a tempting target. Between a second hamburger and refills at the pony keg, I was persuaded to talk to the Sheriff and County Commissioners about the problem on behalf of my neighbors, the victimized East Hills dwellers.

So a sunny summer morning found me, hat in hand, standing before Sheriff DePriest. Speaking as forcibly as possible, I suggested, "Something needs to be done," making strong eye contact. Stan leaned back intimidatingly in a creaky old desk chair, taking a long draw on a big stinky cigar. He carefully looked me over like Clint Eastwood in *Dirty Harry*.

As he reached into the weathered desk, I almost hit the deck, thinking a .44 mag was coming up. Instead, he tossed a weathered, antique deputy sheriff star at me, something likely left over from Bat Masterson and Dodge City.

"Son, you go deal with it! You're now the East Hills deputy," he drawled.

Gary Ziegler, the East Hills Deputy

With a magnetic sign and a "sworn in card" signed by County Clerk Elmer Miller in hand, I drove with apprehension back to the old ranch. This was not quite what I had bargained for. I had acquired EMT certification but knew little about law enforcement.

I had to get up to speed quickly if I was going to seriously

Tools of my new trade

take on this new responsibility. Attending classes at CLETA, the state law enforcement training facility near Golden, I was soon speeding around its obstacle course in a hot pursuit-packaged Ford. Cool stuff. I learned to double tap a bad guy in the vitals at twenty-five yards with the magnum wheel guns (revolvers) then in vogue. Wow!

Having taught climbing and mountain rescue to the Peace Corps, army special forces, and Outward Bound, I did have a background in rescue which was put to use many times during those years.

Needing something more to do, I signed up for the volunteer fire department, training with legendary Westcliffe icons Roger Camper, Leland Niles, Bud Benson, and Dan Riggs. Usually we could only put out the smoldering remains of a structure. Distance to most rural fires prohibited an effective response. We liked to say, "We've never lost a foundation."

I remember Engine #1 was a big, slow, lumbering 1950

Chevy, which I learned to double clutch on. We wore heavy, fire-retardant bunker jackets that would cook you long before anything ignited. Our breathing units were water-soaked bandanas tied around our faces. Technology-wise, we were only a step ahead of the old horse-drawn steam pumpers of a few decades back.

I also drove the county's only ambulance, a modified hearse donated by County Judge and undertaker August Menzel. I guess it was practical, seeing as how it was dual purpose. If the sick or injured didn't make it on the way down the hill to Pueblo hospitals, we just took them back to Augie's Second Street mortuary.

Several years later, around October 1976, Stan suffered a massive heart attack leaving Custer County sheriff-less. By law, the coroner becomes sheriff. My neighbor, Karen Dalby, then coroner and resident MD, was not pleased with this new responsibility. A quickly arranged meeting with the commissioners left me appointed sheriff. I hesitated but oh well.

Here we go.

Using the opportunity to better organize the office, I brought in a friend or two as deputies. A fellow climbing guide and former Town Marshal of Crested Butte, Don West, joined on. An old college acquaintance from Colorado College, Dennis Faulk, was then District Attorney. We worked closely together to close several burglary gangs victimizing the area. Some were local; others came up from Pueblo and Cañon City. Organizing rural residents to report suspicious vehicles and activities, we soon had several thugs locked up and others run out of Dodge.

Two incidents in particular I well remember: The first was a high-speed chase some twenty miles, almost to lowland Rye. It happened one spring afternoon when I was dragging a harrow over the meadow behind an old John Deere B.

Suddenly a strong intuition hit me: Something was wrong. Whipping on a uniform shirt and duty belt, I rolled out from the ranch in the souped-up SUV I drove at the time. Coming out of a driveway near Ilse was a battered convertible pulling a small trailer loaded with household goods.

I hit the lights and punched the siren. The chase was on. Backup? Forget it. The state radio wasn't working. I managed a CB call, which bounced around the county, with me saying, "Breaker, breaker—county mountie needs help—east bound 96."

Fortunately, somebody did get a call to the State Patrol. One daring local even got onto the chase behind me. At one point, I pulled beside the banditos, waving my pistol, but they showed no intention of stopping. Dropping back to avoid endangering oncoming traffic, I followed at a dangerously high speed up and over the winding Bigelow Divide and down the Hardscrabble.

The thieves (we didn't call them suspects then) soon turned off on the dirt Beuleh cutoff, spewing dust and gravel across my windshield. BANG! The convertible blew a tire just as the back seat occupants were attempting to release the trailer. Crashing off the road in a plum of dust—TV, fishing rods, and a typewriter flying—the convertible settled into a big Ponderosa, spewing steam and hostile occupants. I guess they hadn't considered good tires important to their trade.

Pulling an old sawed-off double 12 gauge shotgun, I stepped out. It was a classic *Treasure of the Sierra Madre* stand-off. There were four of them, a tire iron and knives. . . . Would I shoot?

We stared each other down like Gary Cooper in *High Noon*.

Fortunately, I never found out. Just as they started to circle me, the odds shifted favorably. Two State Patrol cars rolled up, followed by the intrepid local. Handcuffs were applied and, yes, we did Mirandize them. Whew! It was another tequila sunset that evening!

I met someone who would become a longtime friend during the trial that followed. Kenny Dresner was a public defender from Pueblo, in those years appointed to represent indigent crooks. Makes sense. If they can't afford tires, they certainly couldn't afford lawyers! DA Dennis and I got a conviction despite Kenny's best efforts. Kenny and I soon became friends. He had never met a rural lawman who knew rules of evidence, one he could not cleverly discredit in court. His unsavory clients went to prison, and we all went out to happy hour.

The second incident was less threatening, but a challenge nonetheless. Local burglars were getting smart. We knew who they were but didn't have the evidence. The pursuit was easy. They drove a truck with mismatched tires. With photos of tire tread taken at the break-ins, we simply wandered around the local Silver Cliff Tavern parking lot at night looking for the right tires. Bingo! There they sat.

The perps (a word we also didn't use then) went out raiding during the day. The subdivisions they preferred had several access roads in and out. Seems they took to posting lookouts with CB radios on hills to report which way we were coming in on patrol.

One day their luck flat ran out!

The suspect truck was reported entering Cristo Vista just over the ridge west of Bear Basin Ranch. Phoning for help from Bear Basin's eight-party line—neighbor Charlie Tomsick was talking at the time—I asked for the line and made the call for help. After, I saddled up my trusted Morgan mare, Bayberry, and headed out the ranch back gate into the subdivision.

Gary with his horse Ouray, responding as the Sheriffs Mounted Posse in 2006

As fate would have it, the first house I came on had the familiar, battered pickup sitting in the drive. I quietly rode up. Barely seconds later, the desperadoes walked out, arms full of loot, straight into twin barrels of the old scatter gun.

"OH SHIT DON'T SHOOT! We ain't done nothing."

I knew these two well enough that I could trust not being challenged. When backup finally arrived, they were face down on the ground with Bayberry and the 12 gauge standing guard, another episode in the passing of the West. Custer County was safe again.

Bringing the story to a close, I did not really relish a lawman career—too much else on the burner—so I gladly stepped down. The commissioners appointed Westcliffe milkman Bob Baker to take over the job until elections came around. Bob was related to almost everyone, so would be a shoo-in come election day. I stayed on as undersheriff for a while, helping to get him up to speed, and then went back to guiding, ranching, cowboying, and sorties to Peru looking for lost cities.

Unfortunately, Bob soon got into trouble in the job. His wife, Lola, bashed a noisy detainee in the mouth with a Rol-a-Tape, a measuring instrument, in the county's new patrol car, landing the Bakers and Custer County in a messy lawsuit.[9] Other problems soon followed.

By the time elections came around, dissatisfaction with Sheriff Bob was pretty much universal. Two former deputies and recently retired Division of Wildlife officer Dan Riggs ran for the office, splitting the vote. Bob remained in office for another four years until he was turned out in the next election.

During those years, tall, lean, guitar-picking, Fred Jobe and his wife, Delores, moved to town. Fred had been a career detective with a large Oklahoma police department. He now took the more laid-back Westcliffe marshal job. Fred was soon elected sheriff. Bob went back to a quieter life with the milk business and later opened a successful liquor store in Silver Cliff with Lola.

Fred became the much respected, long-time sheriff of Custer County. He rode a Harley, sat on a horse, and had a few country music CDs out. Before his retirement, the department was upgraded with twenty-four-hour dispatch, a modern jail, and instant communications.

There's lots more to tell, but this has already grown too long. Maybe some evening around the campfire.

---

[9] See 1983 Civil Rights Case, Max D. Price versus Robert J and Lola M. Baker.

CHAPTER 10

A Memorable Journey on Horseback through Chihuahua's Wild Mountains and Canyons

The summer was 1974. I was running Bear Basin Ranch and had a remuda of half-locoed Appaloosa horses and a string of rangy longhorn cows while occasionally guiding educational programs for Outward Bound and Colorado College in remote canyons of the Sierra Madre. I was very much ready for a good winter adventure.

Thinking about the Sierra, I contacted horse friends who might have interest in a trip there. The final team boiled down to a game gal named Monica and I. We had worked together on the Westcliffe ranch in the Sangre de Cristo range that year. Monica was a very talented horse woman who introduced me to several dangerous activities: fearlessly jumping hyper city horses, show rings, and dry martinis. I showed her cool mountain mornings, cow horses, and slower cowboy ways.

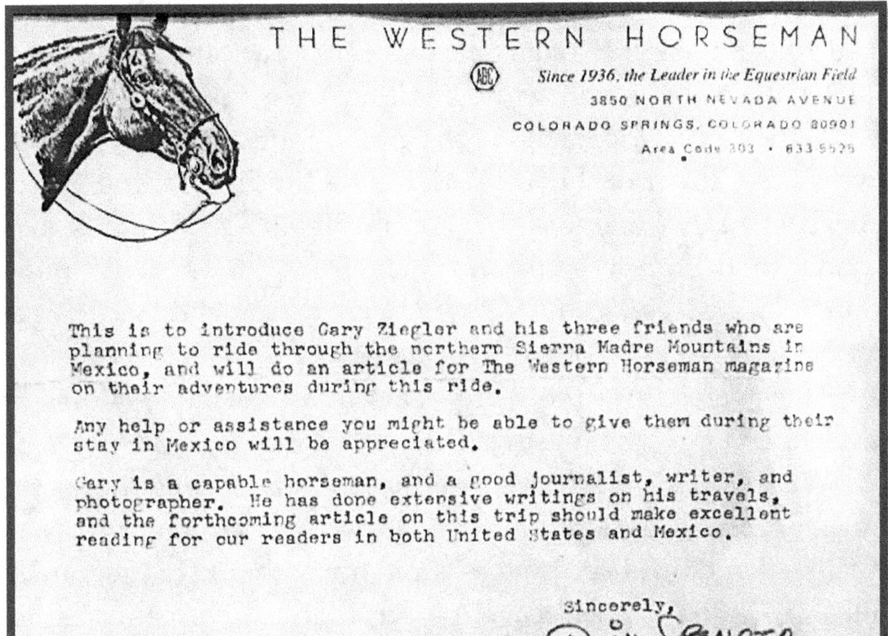

My letter of introduction from Dick Spencer

Dick Spencer, a friend and publisher of *The Western Horseman Magazine*, agreed to sponsor the trip, putting us in contact with Charro friends in northern Mexico for help with finding horses. Finally, with yearlings off to market and the summer horse packing business wound down, we threw two old double-rigged Texas half seat saddles into the back of Monica's ancient station wagon—La Cucaracha my Peruvian friends would call it—driving the long road over Raton, through El Paso, and down to Pancho Villa's old headquarters, the starting place of two revolutions, Chihuahua.

At a rancho outside of town, we popped down $300 for two trail-experienced geldings, Colorado and Moro. They were grade horses, lanky with long, straight heads like the ones in old Pancho Villa photos. We would travel light, with bed rolls and saddle bags and without a pack horse. The old 1880s narrow-tree half seats fitted them perfectly.

Leaving La Cucaracha at the Chihuahua ranch, we set off westward toward the distant Sierra Madre. Riding from rancho to rancho across the rolling plains and foothills, we made good time. We cut and mended a gateless fence now and then but generally followed cow paths and back road tracks that kept on course westward.

This was before the drug years and associated violence that would now make travel there too dangerous.

We had wonderful experiences, treated like honored guests at each village and rancho we passed through. We were fed and our horses were cared for without charge, much like it must have been traveling across the American West in

Monica and Gary in Mexico on our sturdy mounts

the 1800s.

Eventually, crossing back and forth across mountain passes, we arrived to stay with friends at Areponapuchic, a small Tarahumara settlement overlooking the deep Urique Canyon, or Copper Canyon as it is now known to tourists.

This was long before the coming of the road and the big hotels now there. We stayed long enough to rest the horses, treating them to abundant grain. Meanwhile, we feasted on fresh tortillas, refried beans, and roasted goat, putting needed pounds back on our skinny frames.

Then came the real challenge.

Monica and I decided to descend into and cross the big canyon. I had been to the seventeenth-century mining town, Batopilas, some years before. This would be our objective. I knew some of the old Spanish mule routes from our hiking trips with pack burros. Local friends agreed that with extreme care and luck—*mucho suerte*—we probably could get our

**The view into the Urique (Copper) Canyon
from Areponapuchic**

The camp near the river

horses down, cross the rivers, and get up to the high country on the other side.

Most of the routes were seldom used and had been made difficult by floods, slides, and lack of repair. The Tarahumara used them as foot trails or perhaps as pack burro routes between distant ranchos. Riding was out of the question. We led the horses carefully along steep narrow tracks, around washouts, and down slides. Rocks were moved and drop-offs shored up as required.

Eventually we reached the river, making camp on a broad sand beach. Beans, campfire coffee, and a shot of tequila never tasted better. The horses grazed free, not picketed on a long line and a stake as we do in the Colorado mountains. From past experience searching for escapees, we never use hobbles. They don't keep a horse around who wants to leave. In this

Leading my horse along the cliffs

case there was no place for them to go as they feasted on lush green grass in a small wash beside the river. Besides, now we all had bonded such that they considered themselves part of our human herd and we weren't going anywhere far from the campfire.

This was a time before readily available topographic maps and Google Earth. Finding a way out proved to be near impossible. We crisscrossed the river back and forth, both up- and downstream, looking for a way out. Finally we saw a track upward that seemed to have been used recently. Two days later, we climbed five thousand feet and reached the eastern rim only to find yet another deep canyon that unfortunately had to be crossed. I had not been anywhere near here, and it had not been mentioned by the locals back at Areponapuchic.

Once again on foot, we picked our way back down. Several days later we reached impassable cliffs of yellow-stained rhyolite pinching off the canyon. The walls were pockmarked with old shelter caves, smoked pots, corn grinding stones, metates, and wall carvings. We had come upon one of many ancient Mogollon archaeological sites common throughout the canyons.

Here's where the term *short rations* comes into play.

Down to the last tortilla and the coffee pot lost over a cliff, we started back the way we had come with stiff upper lips and empty stomachs. The cliff dwellings were left for another day. Somewhere in the deep canyons they are still out there.

About this time Colorado needed shoes. I dug out a set purchased in a Chihuahua hardware store: horseshoe-shaped flattened metal, three holes to a side, formed from construction re-bar. I fitted them close to right by pounding them with a large rock. Monica's fancy horse friends would have had a seizure.

Colorado may have been ranched trained but apparently no one back at the rancho had been able to shoe him right side up. After a long fight with his feet, which he won, I made a picket rope into a running W, an old cowboy trick for pulling a horse's feet out from under him, putting him down on the ground. The end result was new shoes nailed on, Colorado completely pissed and upside down, and me totally exhausted.

When the dust settled several days later, we were back in the high county following a traveled rim trail. Greeted by passing Tarahumaras, *"Kuira ba,"* we were directed south toward distant ridges. Soon a stop at a small rancho produced welcome beans and better directions.

Monica crossing a stream in the canyon

A week or so later, following an old mule track built to haul out silver from the mines, we rode tall in the saddle into historic downtown Batopilas.

The story goes on.

Some days later, I went over, tangled up with my horse, in the flooding Batopilas River. I was saved by a boot knife. Leaving town, we crossed what I thought was the recommended *vado*, or river ford. This was before the coming of the road and modern bridges some years later. It may have been the *vado*, but a December storm had dumped wet snow in the high country and an inch or two of rain upstream. The raging torrent was too much.

Like a scene from an old John Huston western, Colorado went down and over. I caught a foot in a line coiled among the clutter tied to the saddle. He ended on top, and I ended down as we fought to flee the rapids for high ground. As the story goes, I eventually cut loose and we both swam free. Since then, I always carry a handy knife which has saved my bacon more than once.

Sadly, our cameras and most of the film in the saddlebags went down the Rio Batopilas to the Pacific. That and other events intervened. I never did get the story written up for *The Western Horseman Magazine.* So the story ends, my friends, as an old Ian Tyson song might say.

We made our way roundabout to the rail line, sold the horses, and caught a ride on a locomotive back to Chihuahua on Christmas Eve. Monica and I threw the worn saddles in the battered Cucaracha and headed north toward home.

Pasa la tequila por favor!

CHAPTER 11

The Origins of Custer County
Search and Rescue

When I arrived in 1970, Custer County did not need an organized rescue unit. Sheriff Stan De Priest and his parttime deputies handled the few emergencies. We had one ambulance and the volunteer fire department.

We did have the rare climbing incident on Crestone Needle and a few lost or injured hunters each year. There was almost no backcountry usage except locals going fishing. When there was an issue, Stan would mobilize a few ranchers, usually with horses, for these rare searches or a rescue. If something serious happened on Crestone Needle, the sheriff would contact Alpine or Rocky Mountain Rescue for help, waiting a day or so for them to get here. As backcountry usage increased, it soon became obvious that something more was needed.

As I noted in chapter 9, I was acting sheriff for a time after Stan died in office, presenting an opportunity to better organize emergency service capabilities. There were several climbers living around the county then. We organized a team of climbers who could get quickly up on a mountain—with a radio and an emergency kit to stabilize an injury—and wait for an outside team to arrive. By then, Fort Carson was giving helicopter support, helping to shorten response time in many situations.

Ken Perschbacher had moved to the county some years before. It was Ken's idea to form our own professional, trained search and rescue unit. Ken had started his own construction business, which gave him a flexible work schedule. I attended a meeting Ken organized sometime in the mid-1970s to help get things rolling.

Plaques commemorating Amy's and Gary's service in Custer County's Search and Rescue

Dan Riggs, a local rancher, was the local State Division of Wildlife (DOW) officer. He knew more about trails and hidden places in the Sangre de Cristo Mountains than anyone. Dan had generously shared this knowledge and encouraged me to start my guide and outfitting business some years earlier. He was now a tremendous help and support for the new unit.

Ken followed through with formally organizing Custer

County Search and Rescue (SAR) under the new sheriff, Bob Baker. Dan and I, both overloaded with projects, actively supported the new SAR but did not join. I regularly guided climbers up the Crestone Mountains, which found me involved in a number of rescues. I also led an occasional team when I was available.

One rescue I remember from the mid-1970s stays in my mind. A call came in for a stranded climber in the Royal Gorge. I was the only one available when this call came in from Fremont County, so I threw my climbing gear in the

1926 Postcard of the Royal Gorge
Courtesy of the Library of Congress, LC-DIG-pcrd-1a01643

sheriff department's old four-by-four Scout and raced down Copper Gulch, rooftop red gum ball light ablaze, to the Royal Gorge.

The scene there turned out to be a classic cluster: vehicles, lights, and assorted emergency personnel were everywhere. Ropes, carabiners, and Stokes litters were piled about. However, as it turned out, I was the only one on hand with advanced climbing training and experience.

This was before the days of designated incident command, so as the most knowledgeable operative, I took command. Newspaper accounts pretty much told the story but they missed a few of the stranger details I remember.

Among the equipment clutter, we found several exceptionally long ropes, which allowed me to rappel down hundreds of feet to our stranded airman, twenty-year-old Mike O'Neal. Surprisingly, I found him uncooperative and hostile.

Attaching him with a harness to a belay line, I hooked him onto another rope with jumar ascending devices while I clipped onto a third line. As we began to climb, all was going as smooth as could be expected until some distance up, he became belligerent, refusing to continue. A major scuffle ensued as we swung about on the ropes, dangling above the deep gorge and the Arkansas River below.

After I got a black eye and a few bruises, I managed to incapacitate him with a sort of aerial chokehold. It was indeed a long night before he was eventually hauled up around first light.

I gratefully accepted the mandatory coffee and donut at the mission wrap-up and then drove groggily back to Westcliffe. Airman O'Neal headed home without a goodbye or thanks. I stopped in for breakfast with the morning gang at Susie's Cafe. The local boys politely listened to what could only have been just another Ziegler tall tale.

**Gary leading a rescue up Crestone Needle with
Custer County Search and Rescue**

In the early 1980s, Fred Jobe took office as the new sheriff. Fred and Ken worked closely together to develop a trained and equipped unit. Another retired lawman, Roger McDonnell, moved to the county. Roger became a valuable asset to the SAR team, bringing connections, experience, and energy. Both he and Fred were pilots, keeping planes at Custer County's airfield.

Longtime county resident Art Nordyke was soon involved. Art ran a construction company with heavy equipment and had a passion for snowcats and winter sorties. The unit soon had a team of dedicated winter rescuers equipped with snowmobiles headed up by Art. This, along with a team on skis and snowshoes, added a year-round winter capability.

Another rescue worth mentioning was my last visit to Marble Mountain in August 2005. In the mid-1970s, we had organized a horse packing unit to pack in equipment and for anything else that might be needed. So when a cell phone call came into the sheriff's office on that August day, requesting help for a caver who was injured and in need of evacuation from Spanish Cave at Marble Mountain, we were prepared. Fortunately, I do have an official report of this incident so I can accurately describe the events.

Amy and I gathered our SAR-trained horses and appropriate equipment and then trailered up to the parking lot at the end of South Colony Road, where it becomes a rocky, steep four-by-four road. After several hours of upward riding, we met a small group camped just above the old campsite meadow. The injured party had been successfully extracted from the cave and helped down to the camp. A tough, fit gal named Marty had twisted a knee climbing out of the cave and could not walk. The group had helped her down to the camp the day before. When we arrived, she was in pain but good spirits. She told her story of the accident as the team generously shared their supper with us.

Marty was climbing up the deep shaft near the entrance. Her partner had become chilled and wet going down, deciding to quit the descent. Although comfortable in a wetsuit, Marty decided to accompany her friend. As she swung against a projection something popped in her left knee, leaving her in great pain and with an unusable leg. She was virtually trapped there, halfway up, for several hours.

As fortuitous events happen, a father and his son arrived at just that moment with more rope and pulleys. With help from others outside, she was extracted and was able to crabwalk and slide down to camp.

After a radio conference with the SAR office, we made the decision that a helicopter evac was not necessary. We always tried to avoid helicopters when possible because of the risk created by steep terrain, wind gusts, and altitude. Over the years we have had several helicopter accidents.

Marty believed she could be taken out on horseback. The next morning, we saddled up to begin a careful descent down the old wagon road trail. Amy rode her favorite gray gelding, an extremely trustworthy, sure-footed Paso Fino called Sentinelo. I was riding a big sixteen-hands-high quarter horse appropriately named Ouray, after the famous Ute chief. I was in charge of the Sheriff's Mounted Posse at the time, training and riding the big horse. Ouray had been trained for almost everything: parades, directing traffic in Westcliffe and Pueblo, mountain trail packing, cutting cattle, and most important search and rescue.

With suitable braces and emergency wraps in place, we carefully lifted Marty up onto my secure doubled-rigged old Heiser saddle. I walked along in front, leading Ouray by a lead rope. Several hours later, we arrived safely at the Rainbow Trail, which traverses the base of the east side of the long range. A SAR team was waiting, greeting us with a motorized litter-mounted ATV. Marty went on to treatment and full recovery. She remains involved with caving activities, telling her rescue story on special occasions.

There are so many stories—and so many other SAR members who deserve credit—that I have failed to mention. Everyone who helped form and continues to help run SAR deserves credit. It is an important organization with capable, dedicated, and professional individuals doing important work.

CHAPTER 12

1979—The Year of Living Dangerously

Reflecting back on memorable times and events most influencing the history of Bear Basin Ranch, I am motivated to tell the story of happenings during the eventful winter and summer of 1979–1980. Far distant from our quiet Wet Mountain landscape, our military's special operations, Delta Force, tragically botched a hostage rescue of captured US embassy staff in the wind-blown deserts of Iran.

Closer to home, the wealthy Texas-based Hunt brothers attempted to corner the world's reserves of silver. These were interesting events for discussion in another time and place. I'll come back to the silver fiasco later, as it relates to this story.

In 1979, all was going well at Bear Basin Ranch, for the most part. As iconic folk musician, John Prine wrote, in his song, "That's the Way That the World Goes Round," things were going not bad, we couldn't complain.

Ranch programs were prospering. My official duties with the county had pretty much wound down. As noted earlier, I had been appointed sheriff in October 1976, when Sheriff Stan DePriest died unexpectedly. Not wanting the job permanently, I stayed on until the commissioners appointed local cowboy and milkman Bob Baker to take the job. I officially stayed around as deputy coroner but gave up a volunteer position with the county fire department.

Life then was indeed eventful. As an owner in the founding rafting company on the Arkansas River, Arkansas River Tours, I guided several whitewater runs each month. The horse breeding, training, and trading business in partnership with neighbor Lee Jones was prospering. With a growing ranch staff, we were operating multi-day horse pack trips and guided climbing in the Sangre de Cristo range.

Guiding fourteeners, bringing clients up the difficult Crestone Peaks, we were in demand. I achieved about six ascents each summer season, allowing for a later claim that I held the record with more than one hundred Crestone Needle summitting successes.

My then live-in partner was Deputy County Clerk Joan Lindgren, a very talented horse trainer and skilled organizer. She managed all these programs exceptionally well, including living together in the primitive 1909 ranch office cabin while helping keep County Clerk Mary Kattnig's office organized and efficient.

Joan, a recent Colorado College grad with a degree in geology, had kept connections in numerous places that helped keep a flow of educational and recreational events coming our way. She also helped me with another part-time endeavor: consulting and fieldwork with my dad's company, Ziegler Mining and Minerals.

Sometime in the distant past, along with a degree in philosophy, I had also accumulated four years of geological studies at Colorado College, headed by noted Colorado mineralogist and author Richard Pearl. My dad, Raymond, ran his business with Colorado Springs mining attorney Robert Murray and mineralogist Clarence Coil. Clarence was a founding member of the Pikes Peak Range Riders and a professional photographer.

My dad and his partners owned, leased, and worked a number of regional mining properties. Before the casino tourism boom at Cripple Creek, they had gained control of the defunct United Gold Mines Company, getting access to several abandoned big producer mines.

My first memory of Westcliffe as a child was visiting and collecting samples around the abandoned mine tailings scattered along the White Hills north of town with my folks.

Some of these sites had been worked as recently as the 1940s. Shafts and tunnels stood dangerously open, with weathered head frames still in place. I particularly remember

Gary with his family in front of Silver Cliff Town Hall, circa 1951

several old platform-mounted automobile engines, probably dating from the 1920s, placed to run the hoists.

Some of these tailings, piles of yellowish, Tertiary age, volcanic host rock, can still be seen surrounded by elegant houses and buildings creeping outward from both Westcliffe and Silver Cliff. Nostalgically, I have several bright gold-colored pyrite samples in my inherited family mineral collection from those hills and times.

Later, during a resurgence of exploration for uranium in the late 1970s, I was hired briefly by Cotter Corporation in Cañon City to look for uranium and rare earths in Custer County and the Sangre de Cristos. Supported by our ranch horses, I camped high up in the accessible valleys between Hillside and Music Pass.

Carrying climbing gear, a scintillation radiation counter, and a rock pick, I did a selective radiometric survey of many of the metamorphic layers exposed in canyon walls. It was easy locating radioactive deposits. Uraninite, the oxidized main ore of uranium, occurs locally in dark carboniferous lenses pressed between the tilted, faulted bedding of the Crestone and Sangre de Cristo formations. I located a number of these pancake-like deposits. I also examined a batch of old prospect pits some Silver Cliff boom-era mine seekers had excavated.

In the Sangre de Cristo Mountains, uranium is also associated with copper, which attracted the attention of early prospectors. The fortunate reality saving the natural, undisturbed beauty presented by our valley and mountains today is that none of these deposits were large enough for economically justifiable mining.

Nonetheless, one story tells of how thorium was discovered at Bear Basin around 1947. During the mid-to-late 1940s, various truck crops, particularly potatoes, were grown in the

Wet Mountains area. Upon harvesting, the potatoes were sold to wholesalers in nearby Westcliffe and trucked to various markets by Lee Jones, my neighbor. Lee gave a sack of potatoes from his ranch to his friend Lawrence "Ed" Knobbe.

Both Lee and Ed were from Spearville, Kansas, a small farming community close to Dodge City. The sack of potatoes found its way to Knobbe's home where it was stored in his basement near rock samples he had collected. In checking his rock samples for radioactivity, Ed discovered that the potatoes were radioactive. Ed was able to trace the radioactivity back to the bright red dirt in the eyes of the potatoes. He reconstructed the route traveled by the potatoes and moved to the Wet Mountain area to prospect for the radioactive material, which he assumed to be uranium.

Ed submitted rock samples from Bear Basin and from Haputa Ranch, just south of Bear Basin, to the Atomic Energy Commission. The samples indicated that the radioactivity was due to thorium rather than uranium. In response to Knobbe's discoveries, the U.S. Bureau of Mines drilled the veins and fracture zones at Haputa Ranch in 1951–1952. The only significant ore extracted during the 1950s mining came from our ranches.

My dad and I became partners in buying a ranch near Crystal Peak, north of Florissant, where he and his associates worked a number of pegmatite veins in the hosting Pikes Peak granite. These shallow diggings produced quality green amazonite and smokey quartz crystal specimens, which were sold to collectors and museums around the world. I have a collection of these as well.

Custer County Clerk Mary Kattnig's husband, Floyd, was the County Road and Bridge boss while maintaining a herd of cattle and producing hay at their ranch on Macey Lane. The Kattnigs owned a section of land next to Bear Basin in which

Gary roping cattle at Bear Basin Ranch

I became a partner. Each summer, Floyd and ranch hand Marvin Lang would truck out a batch of cows to the property. I would help manage them until they were taken back to the valley ranch in the fall.

So that was the situation greeting that autumn's fated approach. On the economic horizon, the Hunt's manipulations had sent silver to $50 per ounce. Gold had gone out of sight, closing near a staggering $800 per ounce. Excitement soared among the local mining community. It was a time to re-open properties and pursue new opportunities.

As it happened, I had recently met and become friends with river running enthusiast, Pepe Herrera, in Salida. Pepe came from a well-connected family in Honduras. During happy hour one evening at the town guide's hangout, the historic Victoria bar, we talked about the crazy gold/silver rush underway. He mentioned that he once had found gold in a small river near his home, in the remote cloud forest mountains of Honduras.

Mental light bulbs clicked on.

Over shots of Jose Cuervo, I suggested that maybe we should go to Honduras. Pepe warmed to the idea, telling me more about his family situation and how life could be good on the sunny Caribbean coast. His family owned several large cattle ranches in the mountains and a large meat packing plant in La Ceiba.

By the time we parted that evening, we had cooked up a plan. I would put a team together, raise funding, and purchase equipment. He would handle the arrangements and details needed in Honduras.

I was ready for a challenging new adventure. It was good timing. The river company, managed by co-owner Rick Medrick, was running well without me. Guiding activities and programs at Bear Basin had wrapped up for the season. Joan had decided to move on but would stay at her courthouse job and on the ranch until spring. Floyd and Marvin had retrieved the cows for the winter, and Joan would care for the ranch's remaining herd of horses.

I was good to go!

Now the challenge began. I spent a couple of days in Colorado Springs, staying at my folk's place on the old West Side, not far from downtown. A meeting with attorney Bob Murray, with my dad, and several associates proved encouraging. They would supply the needed funding—a "grub stake" as it was called during the 1870s boom days in Rosita. Next, it was time to put a workable operations and logistical plan together.

Canvassing friends and contacts I thought might be interested, I found two who had the skills, time, personality, and were interested. One was an experienced climbing and river guide I had worked with and trusted, Skip Caldwell. The other was an interesting, successful Colorado Springs business owner who offered to solve a main logistical issue: how to get us and the required tools and equipment to Honduras.

The owner of Don's Cycles, Don Bymaster had a comfortable, bus-size motor home, which he generously offered for travel to Honduras.

Wow, did I jump on that fast!

I had known Don and his wife, Lorena, for many years. They had owned several motorcycle shops in Colorado Springs, and they collected and restored antique aircraft. Don sold me my first motorcycle, a Triumph Tiger Club, around 1956. They would be fun to travel with.

With that important link in place, we began acquiring the equipment needed. We bought two seagoing-sized, inflatable boats with accessories, and I picked up a small portable floating gold dredge. The dredge would be used to suck up river sand, sort out heavier metal particles with an attached sluice platform, and then discard sand back into the water. Finally, we added diving gear and a mounted compressor with a Briggs & and Stratton engine to furnish diver air.

Soon our departure date arrived.

Pepe flew ahead to make arrangements in La Ceiba. Don, Lorana, and I set out southward in the big RV. We stayed several fun days in Mexico City, visiting museums and places of interest. Lorana left us at this point, flying home to attend to business responsibilities.

We continued on to the Guatemalan border with some apprehension. That year had become known as "La Violencia." Thousands had died in the recent civil war. Guatemala was in a state of instability, with unpredictable violence breaking out around the county. Driving the central Pan American Highway seemed like a flashback to driving through the central highlands of Vietnam a decade or so back.

I should mention that we were pulling a large, enclosed trailer loaded with valuable equipment. In sync with the times, we had a hidden stash of guns and ammo. Not only were we a prime target for assault and robbery, but we also were an almost certainty for looting by border guards and frequent roadblock interceptions.

Thanks to my Peace Corps experience and having lived, studied, and worked in South America, I knew the bribery system well. *Mordita,* as it is called in Mexico, saved our bacon. Among important possessions packed in our rig was a box filled with expensive-looking Barbados-made Cuban cigars and packs of real twenty-dollar bills.

Upon being approached by a guard or at a roadblock, I would smile and say, "Buenos Dias Jefe," handing out a couple of cigars and a twenty. This was repeated for all involved. Usually, this was all that was needed.

The guards waved us *adelante* and we were on our way.

As expected, at border crossings and at a couple of other checkpoints, we were asked to open the trailer and the RV for inspection.

The inflatable boats and river items were stacked at the back near the doors. We said we were a river tour company looking for a place to set up to promote adventure tourism. This and a couple of additional twenties miraculously got us through without extensive inspection or required official inventories.

Evaluating the road assault risk, we reluctantly decided to drive at night. We would be less visible and there would be fewer roadblocks. It was a proverbial crap shoot on the unknown odds.

Whew—it amazingly worked!

We arrived at the Honduran border on a sunny, bright Caribbean morning intact and unscathed. The vehicle did reveal a couple of 9 mm-size punctures upon inspection. We jokingly called them road hazard damage.

We then drove on to La Ceiba, a quiet, picturesque fishing community on Honduras's Caribbean coast. In those archaic times, communication was limited to telegrams, mail, or a phone booth. There were no practical means to contact Pepe. We could only hope he was there and had arrangements in place. Equally primitive, we had to rely on a paper road map to navigate. There was no pleasant female voice coming from a dash-mounted heads-up display saying, "Turn right in one quarter mile."

By late evening we arrived at the address Pepe had given us. It pleasantly turned out to be a very comfortable, modern, large bungalow located on the town's golf course. Pepe cheerfully greeted us with bowls of fruit, grilled steaks, and a round of freshly squeezed orange juice laced with ample local top-shelf rum.

Not a bad ending to a long trying journey!

We slept conformably, safe and relaxed in elegantly furnished, mosquito-netted rooms. Tomorrow would bring a new adventure, as Willie and Waylon prophetically sang that year in their song, "Mammas, Don't Let Your Babies Grow up to Be Cowboys."

Following a few days of sightseeing, meeting Pepe's family, visiting their extensive meat packing complex, and general relaxation, we settled into serious planning. Don enjoyed the week and then prepared to go home. The Colorado Springs business required his return. He had not planned to participate in the prospecting, so we were on track for his leaving. The RV was serviced, got a new tire, and was pronounced good to go by the Herrera mechanics.

The only discomforting aspect was that Don would have to run the gauntlet back through Guatemala and Mexico alone, with no backup drivers. It speaks of his adventurous spirit and courage. He was a great and much appreciated contributor to our off-the-wall project. We solemnly saw him off, vehicle loaded with crates of choice local food, mandatory dollars, and cigars. The trailer was left for project use and would be sold later.

It was wonderful news when we received a message through a La Ceiba ham radio network operator that Don had arrived home safely. He had successfully made it through Guatemala without being shot. The only mishap he mentioned was damage to the bus from striking a cow at night somewhere near Zacatecas. It would be a test of the travel insurance policy.

Our preparations slowly came together. The first item was trying to determine where we were going. Pepe remembered that his river of gold was somewhere in the mountainous cloud forest northwest of San Pedro Sula. We looked through air navigation charts and the few topo maps available—without success. Next we spent a day flying the area in a chartered Cessna 172.

Finally, Pepe thought he had found it. "There it is—that's it—that small canyon below." He remembered looking for lost cattle with his uncle there many years before. A primitive single-track road could just be seen leading to a small, almost overgrown clearing beside a small river. It all looked logistically feasible.

Grabbing Skip upon our return, we celebrated that evening with juice and rum concoctions, freshly caught fish, and dancing with a couple of Pepe's lady friends at a dockside bar. To local delight, I pounded out a couple of old ranch cowboy ballads on a borrowed bar guitar. After several rums, I even managed a verse or two of "El Rancho Grande, Allá Donde Vivía."

Moving on, Pepe came up with a couple of four-by-four trucks, several helpers, a few small ATVs, and camping gear. With our loaded expatriated Colorado trailer in tow, we set out for the distant wilds of northwestern Honduras.

Later that week, after arriving at the spot, we managed to assemble a working diver-supported floating dredge on the small river. We had also set up a reasonably comfortable camp not far away. We had previously tested the rig on the Arkansas River below Salida, so we knew it would work. That test proved valuable as we tried to get the rig up and running.

Here is how it worked.

The dredge floated on inflated pontoons. It had a small gasoline engine powering a suction unit. Attached was a flexible long, wide hose, which sucked up sand from the river bottom. The sand and water then routed over a shaking, elongated platform before returning to the river. This created a process of weight differential separation. Heaver particles like gold and silver were separated and retained.

Facilitating this operation necessitated one of us directing and holding the hose underwater at the best potential sand

A floating dredge

deposits. To accomplish this, we had a sort of jury-rigged system that professional divers would have freaked out about.

Installed on the accompanying boat was another small gasoline engine powering an air compressor with a long hose. One of us would be underwater directing the suction hose. The air hose would be attached to a regulator held on by a modified climbing harness and then routed up to a mouthpiece breather and face mask. Skip and I would regularly change places—one of us in the water and the other running the compressor in the boat.

Eureka!!

We had collected only a small amount of gold. However, quantities of something else we were recovering was assayed in San Pedro Sula: silver carbonate. Wow—silver was trading at around $50 per ounce!

Then disaster struck.

After several weeks of operation, the dredging rigs were sitting about a half mile upstream from the roadbed camp. Late one night, the proverbial shit hit the fan. Two vehicles loaded with heavily armed desperadoes roared into camp. We were armed but not able to deal with this. We were held captive while the camp was looted. After a bit of Pepe's private negotiation, we were allowed to enter our trucks and drive away with a warning: "Do not come back."

As Kenny Rogers sang in his song, *The Gambler*, it was time to fold up and get out of Dodge.

We took that advice by driving northward back to La Ceiba. It took a few days of quiet rest at the Herrera bungalow to recover from what was a narrow escape from almost certain death. All was not so bad. We had been able to retrieve the bags of collected ore, which Pepe had prudently kept stored in a family safe house in San Pedro Sula. We still had a remaining boat, an extra compressor, and dive gear left in La Ceiba. Although we were almost eaten alive by the country's notorious sand fleas, we still had our lives and good health to be thankful for.

Several months remained before I needed to head home for the ranch and business demands summer would bring. Pepe had our ore processed at a refinery in Tegucigalpa, leaving us with a considerable amount of silver and a small quantity of gold after he extracted his share. We would take the remainder home for sale there and distribute it to our investors.

With free time and available resources on hand, Skip and I decided on a new adventure. Loading the boat and dive gear on a ferry, we headed out to the nearby island of Roatan.

At this point I should share a bit on what was going on politically in Central America during those unsettled times. I have mentioned the year of "La Violencia" in Guatemala. Honduras, with some exception, was relatively stable at the moment. Neighboring Nicaragua was in a complete state of disaster. An armed insurgency, the Sandinistas, had just overthrown the decades-old Somoza dictatorship. The Sandinistas were quickly backed by geopolitics, being influenced, funded, and armed by the Soviets, Cuba and you-name-it leftist sources. A counterinsurgency called the Contras was forming. It began training in remote areas of Honduras and Costa Rica.

Although not officially supported by the United States, this group would become secretly funded by clandestine elements of our government. This would become a political scandal during the Reagan administration, involving the sale of weapons through intermediaries to Iran with the profits being channeled to the Contras in Nicaragua. For more on this, it is worth looking up Oliver North and the Contra affair.

I mention the situation as it directly relates to our experiences in Honduras. The group that attacked our camp were likely Sandinistas, who operated small groups attempting to destabilize the country. Honduras remained sympathetic to wealthy Nicaraguan landowners and merchants, encouraging them to transfer assets to Honduras.

These events were affecting Roatan. The narrow estuary leading into the ferry dock was filled with fishing boats, small freighters, tugboats, and several luxury yachts that had arrived recently from Nicaragua to avoid seizure. I remember someone saying, "That's Somoza's fishing fleet over there."

The first evening, meeting a couple of fit-looking Americans in the local waterfront bar, we shared a couple of Carib beers over fish and chips. The conversation turned to what we all were doing in Roatan. After an exchange of somewhat unlikely explanations, I realized that these guys were likely CIA operatives. What cemented an interesting candid association was that they had been with Fifth Special Forces Group in Vietnam.

What established my credentials and authenticity was that I knew the group commander, John Kelly, who now was retired and living in Denver, and that I had been attached to the unit in the late 1960s. I also had had some involvement with a few CIA special operations. So we were invited to bunk nearby on a company-owned trawler. More exciting, we were invited for a stay at their quietly leased headquarters, called appropriately the Inn on Spy Glass Hill, a luxury resort above a remote bay.

It is time to end this story. Skip and I briefly became lobster fishermen, using our unique diving rig brought from La Ceiba. Going out to the many nearby shallow reefs, one of us would run the compressor while the other dived below to retrieve lobsters from reef depressions. Locals taught us to use a long hook-ended rebar to pull the lobsters out of their hideouts. We would then trade the catch for supplies back in town.

As spring was coming on, it was time to think about returning to Colorado and Bear Basin. Skip caught a ferry to the mainland and a flight to Colorado. I stayed on for another month or so, taking a job as first mate on a charter fifty-one-foot Morgan Out Island ketch sailing the Bay Islands for Caribbean Yacht Charters.

Aww—the Fickle Finger of Fate.

Leaving the boat and gear with Pepe, I boarded a local flight to Tegucigalpa, loaded down with a bag of silver bars and a small amount of gold. Flying from there to Miami was the last flirt with danger. I took one of the last perilous Lockheed Electras still flying. Then it was home to Colorado on a safer US airline. It was about then that gold and silver values crashed; Silver Thursday, March 27, 1980, bought silver down to around $11 per ounce. Our great Honduras project went from extremely profitable to near disaster.

The good news was that after distribution, the investors broke even, and I had had a great winter getaway.

CHAPTER 13

Voyage of the Ketch *Pleiades*

Custer County Crew Survives an Epic Sailing
Adventure Around Far Panama

"What's that ugly black wall of cloud out to the north?" Approaching the Escudos anchorage, a violent rain squall slams hard in on us. Visibility drops to zip. Sails are dropped and the engine is started. Engaging forward, the shift lever comes off in my hand. On both sides of us we hear the pounding breakers.

In November 2009, old friend and Peru expedition partner Nick Asheshov and I talked about moving his two sailboats from Bocas del Toro near the Costa Rican border down to a more central marina at the Panama Canal. Nick and his wife, Maria del Carmen, lived in Peru's famous Sacred Valley, where they owned a railroad serving Machu Picchu. Nick is a yachtsman who loves the occasional sailing getaway, hence the desire to have the boats stashed in Panama. Unfortunately, his two wonderfully restored classic older vessels had been neglected by a less than responsible facility contracted to keep them ship shape.

Always looking for an excuse to sail, I eagerly agreed to oversee the project. Canvassing (no pun intended) sailing friends, we ultimately pulled together a crew of my partner and future wife, Amy Finger, and Westcliffe friend, Lynn Prebble, a gal who has climbed Mount Everest and can handle whatever comes along. We have all sailed together through very rough seas. Although Amy was handicapped by a recent serious illness, I had confidence that the three of us could successfully handle the forty-eight-foot ketch *Pleiades* through whatever fate threw at us. And, as could have been predicted, fate did not let us down.

Pleiades

The ominous start was a tropical depression hanging over Panama, predicted to become hurricane Ida the day we were scheduled to arrive. However, as it turned out, the weather was clear and sunny for several days before turning to endless rain squalls. Winds were light and mostly coming bow-on at us or dead astern. Sailing the thirty-six-year-old Florida-built Soverel ketch proved indeed a challenge.

She had been completely refurbished in Cartagena some three years back, but unfortunately, not much now worked. The sails were stained but good. All the lines were weak and frayed. We replaced most and did manage to get all sails up on occasion. The hatches leaked badly, keeping us soaked below decks much of the time. The charts were outdated and frequently just wrong. Radar and VHF were dead. We depended on a hand-held GPS, my hand radio, and luck. The stove worked only if someone on deck shook the propane tank every few minutes. The DC to AC inverter had walked away during storage at Bocas del Toro, leaving no way to charge our cell phones or the portable VHF radio. Therefore, we only turned these on when needed, resulting in no one being able to contact us. Fortunately, a handful of AA batteries could keep the GPS going.

On the plus side, the fridge was great. It made ice and kept all items cold. We always had chilled vodka and rum. The solar-charged battery system never faltered, although most lights, and all but one of the cabin fans, failed. The boat's best feature was a dependable, almost new Yanmar 100-horsepower turbocharged diesel engine. Up front, the boat carried a sixty-pound CQR anchor and 150 feet of chain. We had a big fortress backup anchor as well. I was confident we could drop these and hold through almost anything and more. The almost new windlass hauled it all up when so tasked!

The stay at Bocas del Toro, where we picked up *Pleiades,*

was fun—nice folks and good food, not too expensive. We bought a well-used 5-horsepower outboard cheap, so we did not have to paddle about in the dingy. It finally failed at our last port of call but was not needed after that. We sailed off, in the wake of Nick's local friend Daniel—an ex-pat Peruvian with a trimaran—through tricky shoaled passages to his place on a small island, Cayo del Agua.

Daniel had his own little cove with a small dock, palms, and thatched huts. It felt like something out of a Hollywood *Treasure Island*. The water was emerald green, and the island was covered in tropical vegetation with high volcanic rocks projecting steeply skyward to form the boundaries of the cove.

After hooking up to a dubious-looking moss-covered mooring—Daniel assured me it was good—we used the dingy to go around to a deserted white sand beach for a much-needed run before happy hour. That evening, Daniel fired up his BBQ grill, serving up fresh tuna we had bought in Bocas del Toro. We started with sushi marinated in soy and hot wasabi sauce followed by lightly grilled tuna fillets. Rum with assorted juices was the adult beverage of choice for the occasion.

The following morning broke calm, hot, and sunny. Daniel directed us out on a complicated route through reefs, leading to the big tanker port, Chiriqui Grande, for fuel and the required official sailing papers, something called a *zarpe*. As we parted, he casually commented that we'd "have no problem—just follow the deep water as it winds around shoals." It seemed he used a GPS navigational system with built-in new charts that steered for him. Plus, his boat drew only a couple of feet. *Pleiades* drew six.

With Amy shouting course changes extracted from our alleged GPS location on the ancient chart, we wound around, trying to follow the serpentine channel. Lynn stayed out on the bow pulpit and kept pointing at visible shallows and obstacles as I watched the gyration of the depth sounder. Several times, I put the wheel hard over, hitting high revs or a hasty reverse. After a stressful few hours of down to less than a foot of water under the keel, we dropped anchor and fortunately got Daniel on the cell phone (it was the last place it worked). He came out in the trimaran to lead us through to the main channel.

"What's the matter with you guys, can't you navigate?" he hollered.

That evening, we dropped hook at the port, but it was too late for officialdom or fuel. The next day turned out to be a national holiday, so all offices were closed. However, in proper Banana Republic tradition, a few extra dollars opened the port office. Fuel had to be brought to us by guys in canoes. Although massive tankers were unloaded here, the local municipal fuel dock was too shallow for us. Diesel was a modest $3 per gallon plus $15 to have it delivered. Not a bad deal considering what we regularly paid out in the eastern Caribbean. We took on forty gallons, which I figured now gave us a good sixty in the tanks, enough for about three days of engine running.

Should be enough to see us through to the Panama Canal.

The town folks were friendly and helpful. Lynn shopped for a few additional items, like missing life jackets—she found some at twelve bucks each. I did the official stuff spending about $60, along with several hours, signing forms, copying ship papers, and showing passports. Finally, we secured the needed *zarpe*.

We were good to go.

It turned out private boats were not welcome there, so we were told to hit the road ASAP. Apparently, the oil company folks worried a lot about terrorists and sabotage.

Meanwhile, the weather had turned ugly, but we had to go. When the dingy motor failed, we were left with a difficult paddle back to the boat in a screaming squall. The depth sounder chose that moment to quit. More on that to come. The squall was so bad that I could hardly find the huge channel buoys leading out of the place. Trusting the binnacle compass and ancient chart (Balboa probably had a better one), we set off for the open seas.

It was now late in the day, and I was wondering where we could hole up for the night. We were heading out between shallow reef-lined islands in a deep ship channel, not that we could tell with the defunct deep sounder. The yellow, water-stained chart showed something reasonable looking to star-board called Bluefield Bay. A quick computation suggested that we could make this bay just before dark. We furled in the sails. Putting the throttle to the stops as a black squall ham-mered us, we approached the bay. With minimal visibility and no depth gauge, I eased her in close to a headwall up a small bay. Lynn let the anchor fly and there we were.

Amy cracked the wine. Lynn poured a vodka, complete with olives, and handed it to the over-stressed skipper. In-tense rain hammered the deck, but I was just happy to be safely at anchor, wherever we might be.

Morning greeted us gray and raining. I wondered which was wetter, the aft cabin or the deck. Lynn somehow man-aged to brew a pot of strong coffee from the reluctant galley stove. We stumbled up into the cockpit, coffee in hand, and listened as tropical birds and howler monkeys squawked pro-tests at the weather. We silently agreed.

During our last correspondence with Nick, it was agreed that he and Maria del Carmen would meet us today at Shelter Bay Marina at the Colón end of the canal. But we knew we weren't going to make it. No way were we willing to put out to sea in the midst of a storm and with no weather information. Moreover, we had no communication. *Pleiades* had an old single-side band radio on board, but based on the other electronics, I doubted it would work. Plus, I didn't know the working frequencies and hadn't used one in more than twenty years. My diminutive, handheld VHF had a range of less than twenty miles.

Cell service? Forget it.

Remarkably, by midday the weather had cleared. We found ourselves in a delightful, remote small bay riding gently at anchor. We were located just off a small beach with palm trees and assorted tropical exotics, fronted by underwater coral formations.

All of us jumped overboard.

Lynn and Amy headed for the coral while I drove the dingy. I saw there were a couple of feet of water under the keel. Not bad for coming in blind. My biggest concern was the defunct depth sounder. I checked the hull outlets that might have sucked in items, but all were clear. Heading back to the sailboat, I attempted a re-calibration of the sounder unit. It was running completely amok. When I turned it on, it read one and a half feet. Then, with regular and precise movements, it increased one foot at a time until it reached seventy feet. Then it again went down to one and a half feet. I tried various procedures—none helped—but a good pounding on the deck seemed to finally cure the malfunction. I remounted it and was pleased to see it now read a true and continuous two feet.

Whew! Hopefully it would keep working!

Back on board the gals reported seeing brilliantly colored coral and a large assortment of fish, particularly one big spotted fellow. We could see small rays everywhere. The chart said we were actually in Bayo Rayes. At least the chart makers got something right. Now with us somewhat dried out and with land visible, we decided to explore the rest of Bluefield. It looked to be about three miles up to the end, with a number of small fishing huts scattered along the shore. We cranked in the anchor, motored out and then inland—soon easing carefully into shallows near the head of the long bay. I always like to anchor a good distance offshore to avoid night visitation of airborne insects, so we dropped anchor about two hundred meters out in eight feet of water.

There were canoes and small motor launches coming and going around us from the small hamlets, pleasantly paying us no attention except a polite wave. It became one of those magical anchorages. The water was mirror surface calm. The sky was crystal clear, filling later with a multitude of bright stars. We shared drinks and talked ancient philosophy, finishing up with a near gourmet dinner on deck while the gentle flicker of oil lights and candles reflect from the shore.

Early the next morning, we pulled up the anchor and pointed the bow seaward. Amy had laid out our course and way points. The plan was to sail west a few miles out of Bluefield Bay, around some nasty breaking rocks called Los Tigres, and then come to course slightly north of east. Strangely, the Isthmus of Panama runs east–west. One expects that sailing off Central America, we would head south, but that wasn't what we were doing.

The wind was mild out of the west, with a gentle rolling sea. We rounded the Tigres, killed the engine, and popped up all the sails. A slightly clocking breeze of around ten knots pushed us astern. We got *Pleiades* balanced wing to wing, the big Genoa all the way out and filled. The mizzen boom was laid over hard, giving drive as well. Running with an easterly current, we made six and better knots. Nick had reported that the old Robertson autopilot was unreliable, but to my delight, I got it up and working.

Yes—it could even handle the wallows of a broad reach.

By late afternoon, we had clicked off the distance to our rest stopover at a small island called Escudo del Veraguas, some twenty miles off Panama's sparsely populated Mosquito Coast.

What's that ugly black wall of cloud out to the north? I wondered. Approaching the Escudo anchorage, a violent rain squall slammed hard in on us. Visibility dropped to zip. Sails were quickly dropped and the engine was started. Engaging forward, the shift lever came off in my hand. On both sides of us we heard the pounding breakers.

Where we were looked too deep to drop anchor. We were being set hard over down-wind when the prop locked in neutral. For what good it would do, Lynn took the helm as I rushed below to the engine room. I found a headlamp and pliers in the dark pitching space, which was beyond luck. I followed the control cables to a lever on the side of the transmission case forward of the propeller shaft. Remembering that back was really forward on the binnacle control, I pushed the lever down. The shaft began to turn, hopefully in the right direction, although by then I would have been happy to have propulsion in any direction.

If it happened to be reverse, we would have made that work.

Rushing up, I took the helm and advanced the throttle. Yes! We moved forward against the set. About that time, the sky cleared some, affording a view of where we needed to go. Amy had a GPS point located as well. We carefully motored in and found a shallow place to drop our anchor while we killed the engine.

Escudo was touted as a protected overnight stop for those

traveling up and down the Panama coast, but no way could we rest here. The boat went immediately sideways to the incoming rollers, pitching almost rail to rail. Meanwhile, a small launch, out of who knows where, pulled alongside us. Two unsavory characters demanded $10 and beer to anchor there. I came up from the cabin with three ones and a flare pistol stuck in my shorts. I told them we were leaving and had no beer. They looked me over, took the $3, and grudgingly pulled away.

Amy somehow magically produced a delicious tuna sushi with tossed (no pun intended) salad. We enjoyed the light dinner before Lynn wound in the anchor. I started the engine and off we headed on an all-night cruise. The weather looked a bit unsettled, but we had no options.

The sea calmed down as we rounded the leeward side of the island once again on the easterly course. Sails were sheeted for a following wind as darkness crept over the horizon.

Happiness was Escudo in the rearview mirror!

Solitude and tranquility, a calm night at sea under bright stars. As stars broke out of the light clouds, we settled into a pleasant night sail. Amy slept below in the big aft cabin with the aft companionway open to the cockpit. She continued to run a half hour position and course plot. Lynn and I shared the watch, dosing on deck with the celestial Pleiades gleaming overhead. Old Uncle Auto, with only occasional course tweaking, had the helm.

After traveling some seventy miles, we had the seas completely to ourselves. We saw only one small light somewhere off the coast during the twelve hours of darkness. Dawn cleared with a calm sea, allowing coffee and breakfast up from below. *Pleiades* was still making a solid six knots on course into the rising sun.

By early afternoon, we saw many large ships looking like tall skyscrapers on the horizon. Around one o'clock we sailed casually through some twenty-plus anchored ships of every size and configuration lying off the mega port, Colón.

Two long breakwaters stretched out in a V, seaward from Colón's Limon Bay, leaving a five-hundred-foot-wide gap: the Atlantic entrance to the Panama Canal. Inside the immense bay, we saw more anchored ships, either awaiting passage through the locks or having already been through from the Pacific side. We made a dash through the gap between massive outbound container ships and followed a marked channel back westerly inside the breakwater that led to Toro Point and Shelter Bay. Amiable South African Dock Master Dave Jerling was expecting us at the marina. With no reverse, we eased alongside the big boats dock until a slip could be found for us.

Relieved, Nick finally reached us on the cell phone. He and Maria del Carmen were in Panama City and on their way out to greet us.

The journey ended. We spent several more rainy days at the marina evaluating and preparing *Pleiades* for storage. We eagerly moved to dry, comfortable rooms in the new Marina Hotel. Later, Lynn and I moved *Pleiades* to the hauling dock and rode her out of the water to be stored ashore. Nick, Dave, and I completed a careful inspection. The hull looked good. Steam-cleaning revealed a few small osmosis spots but nothing serious. The rudder was holed and needed sealing. The carrier bracket for the propeller shaft needed replacement and the shaft shortened.

We were pleased to find her in such okay condition.

However, a long list of repairs and replacements would keep her shore-bound for some time. She needed new hatches and seals, the teak oiled, new electronics, and a thorough refit.

The grand old gal deserved the best! We stayed the last night in the city with friends Brian and Margarita Riley, who had recently moved to Panama from Westcliffe, Colorado. Brian was heading the Panama Peace Corps project. He was about the best source of regional events and cultural information that could be found. A long day's flight home was uneventful, and Colorado greeted us with freezing temperatures.

The final question of the trip: will Nick sell *Pleiades* or do we plan the next epic voyage? The seldom-visited San Blas Islands lie just a long day's sail away.

So the story ends. For now

CHAPTER 14

Christmas Cows at Bear Basin

It was 2009 and I was leading a small group to view the winter solstice sunrise illuminating what I believed was a prehistoric ceremonial site on the promontory overlook above our 1870s ranch house. Suddenly we came upon one of the ranch cows staring at us from a clearing beneath a big pine. At her side was a just born calf!

"Hey Tuft, what are doing up here?" I yelled as we tromped uphill through old ponderosas and a recent snow covering the trail. Cows never go up here in the winter and certainly never alone.

Tuft was an elderly Hereford that we had kept around in retirement. Several years back she had suffered a prolapsed uterus making her sterile, or so our vet said. She had not calved since then, but now here she was with a healthy calf born just minutes before we got there.

Old Tuft and her solstice baby

We had always planned breeding for late spring calves. Old Tuft was left accompanying a young bull all summer in her much-earned retirement. Here was an unplanned and wonderful result.

Solstice morning and Christmas week—we never go up there in winter yet now here we were. And here we found Tuft and a tiny miracle. The coincidence was staggeringly mystical to me.

That thought went through my head as we continued our hike toward the prominent Pleiades star cluster and a vertically aligned Orion's belt over the distant western horizon. We must have metaphorically resembled the mythological three wise men following a guiding star to Bethlehem.

119 degrees
shaped
Dec. solstice sunrise 2019
Bear Basin Ranch
shaped
G Ziegler 2019

SANGE DE CRISTO MOUNTAINS
SHAPED PINES
AND FIRST ILLUMINATION
DECEMBER SOLSTICE SUNRISE
BEAR BASIN RANCH
G ZIEGLER

Returning to reality, I knew we were not bringing "gifts of great joy,"—not gold, frankincense, and myrrh—only cameras, iPhones, and compasses. And yes, the sun arrived as predicted to illuminate a path directly through a pair of strategically placed and bent ponderosas, indicating that spiritually minded ancients had been here before us.

A round of holiday parties and a family gathering followed that mystic morning. Whew—we at least decided on a quiet Christmas home alone. The old kitchen range at the ranch house was going all day, stoked with coal and split aspen, the ancient oven holding a steady 350 degrees. Amy found a select prime rib roast at the local Westcliffe market and marinated it in Worcester sauce, wine, and secret spices. She stuck in a thermometer and slid it into the heated iron orifice.

Meanwhile, I piled on heavy clothes and pulled two less-

Home at the Bear Basin Ranch

than-enthusiastic horses from the remuda. The horses had been happily munching around the feeders and weren't excited as I saddled them up.

Temperatures were hovering around zero.

As the evening meal cooked, we set off to feed hungry stock at a neighbor's place. Our neighbors were away visiting warmer environments for the holidays. Our unshod ponies had to break through a few sizable snowdrifts, but they settled into a strong working stride and took us dependably there through a blowing ground blizzard.

Returning late—cold, tired and very hungry—Amy pointed out that one of our cows was away from her compadres and standing underneath a distant pine. I unsaddled, turned out the ponies, and went out to investigate as Amy saw to the gastronomic preparation inside.

From here, I'll let Amy tell the story.

"On the last stretch in, I noticed a cow by herself under a ponderosa and asked Gary to go check on her. He did. She had just broken water with a small foot emerging. This cow was due much later but obviously was calving early with no warning. Gary thought she would need help and came back to tell me.

"As I still had only limited use of my left arm, Gary said, "let's call the neighbors." Gary called Hal and Mary Walter, who were just sitting down for their Christmas dinner. They in turn called another neighbor, Nancy Hedberg, well-known for her animal husbandry skills. Nancy promptly offered to come over. Her husband, Pete, was cooking Christmas dinner, so she fortunately had some time.

"Our own prime rib was now perfectly cooked medium-rare sitting on the warming shelf, my corn and green chili souffle bubbling in the oven.

"Nancy arrived—carrying her packed mid-wife duffle bag

—complete with towels, frozen colostrum, a nursing bottle, and a pulling rope. She brought her daughter, Megan, who had just pulled a calf as part of a 4H project. They evaluated our cow, who they dubbed Mother Mary.

"The feet were pointed the right direction, and we could see the tongue and head emerging, so all was sort of well. However, this two-year-old first-calf heifer was having trouble pushing out what was obviously a very big calf. Nancy got a rope around the protruding foot and began pulling.

"Mother Mary was very receptive and seemed to understand we were trying to help. She was just standing free in the barn, not restrained in any way, allowing us to work on her. Finally, another foot emerged. Nancy lassoed that one as well. Gary pulled in tandem with Nancy. I stood safely behind the gate, shining the light. (It was now well past dark and in the single digits, temperature wise.)

"Mother Mary was in agony, and she flung herself around the barn, hitting the walls and Gary. After what seemed like forever, with the calf's head squeezed into the birth canal, the calf finally popped out during a well-timed contraction coupled with fierce pulling.

"Miraculously, the calf, a healthy heifer, was alive and began sucking on Nancy's fingers. She had been birthed with an incredibly thick winter coat of hair, well prepared for the weather. I threw Nancy towels and she dried the calf off while Gary spread a thick, clean layer of straw down in the corral. We made sure Mother Mary got up and started licking her babe. Gary lifted the baby to the teat, where it greedily took to nursing."

The Christmas calf was alive and safe, Amy and I hurried back to our warm kitchen, and she rescued the overcooked souffle. Over celebratory drinks, we gave thanks for our newborn Christmas gift—a reminder of another manger and birth

Little Navidad meets his neighbors as Mother Mary watches.

in a far-off time and land. After Nancy and Megan left for their own dinner, Amy made an awesome gravy from the roast drippings. Finally, the eagerly anticipated Christmas dinner was ready to be served!

The next morning little "Navidad," as we named her, was following her mama around the corral.

All was well.

It was a perfect cowboy Christmas.

CHAPTER 15

Memorable Happenings: 1980 to Present

The adventures, events, and meanderings collected in previous chapters are not complete without a chapter about life with my wife, Amy Finger Ziegler, and the amazing happenings she initiated, supported, and contributed to.

It began sometime in the early 1970s. Amy's remarkably talented family—her engineer-trained dad, schoolteacher mom, older brothers, and sister—purchased a lot nearby in newly established Cristo Vista. In harmony with the times, they decided to build an alternative, trendy, Buckminster Fuller geodesic dome as a summer residence. I remember meeting Amy as the dome was being built.

We all soon became friends. Amy's brothers, Mark and Jeff, hosted great summer parties, many of which I attended. Sometime in the late 1970s, Amy and I re-connected. Amy stopped by and asked about going on one of our day rides on the ranch. My then girlfriend, ranch manager Joan offered a creative exchange. Amy could have a free ride if she would help us put up hay that week. She did just that. A day or two after the haying was finished, we saddled up several ranch Appaloosas and rode to the dome and back.

The day ended pleasantly. We shared a cookstove dinner in the ranch bunkhouse while I picked out a few campfire favorites on my old Gibson guitar with Amy and Joan singing along. Amy headed back to college studies in Iowa that week. We lost track as lives and events moved on.

In 1980, Amy tried to contact me about working for the ranch. I had been in Honduras that winter (see chapter 12) and didn't get her letter until I returned in April. I asked Joan, who was then moving on to Grand Junction, if she remembered what Amy's experience was. She was uncertain but recommended I call her. When Amy finally got through on the always busy eight-party telephone line, she convinced me that I could use her help to get the riding business up and running that summer.

Amy arrived in May, driving in on a battered old Dodge Dart with her dog Gabriel. The old ranch buildings reminded her of her favorite place in Iowa, her great-aunt Ruth's cottage, which had no running water or electricity. She recalled, "It was a beautiful, simple place in the countryside."

Amy had childhood memories of washing her hair with a ceramic pitcher and basin outside and starting fires in an old potbelly stove. Eighteen-year-old Amy was far more interested in the ranch than in me, an old man of thirty-eight at that time.

Together we advertised for and interviewed wranglers. I had a significant amount of business booked through marketing agencies, and we needed help! We cooked dinners together and played chess during the lengthening spring

Gary and Amy riding with friends on the ranch

evenings prior to assembling a crew. We hired some great characters, like fiddle-playing Lauren. Amy, an orchestral violinist since elementary school, taught Lauren how to read music in exchange for learning to fiddle and play by ear. Amy, Lauren, and I, with my guitar, would jam with local players at the Lake DeWeese clubhouse on weekend nights. Then, suddenly, all of us were so busy with ranch business that we could barely keep up. The summer passed quickly.

Later, firewood in, hay cut and stacked, we turned to training horses as a winter project. We had another wrangler named Bev who was a very talented horsewoman. Neighbor Lee Jones also got involved, offering his round pen and advice at the old Jones house. Of course, he wanted his young colts worked as well. We trained up some fine horses, buying more from Lee, creating a good-sized remuda for the next summer.

Amy had planned to stay for only that one summer, but she fell in love with working the horses and taking horse pack trips in the Sangre de Cristo wilderness, so she stayed on at the ranch. As fate would have it, by June we were living together in my turn-of-the-century ranch cabin. Sometime over the winter she had decided that this ancient thirty-eight-year-old guy might be okay as a partner. Moreover, I could occasionally even beat her at chess!

By 1981, Amy had established her residency in Colorado,

Amy with her dog Gabriel on Comanche Pass Trail during the summer of 1980

which qualified her for Pell grants for tuition to attend the University of Colorado in Colorado Springs the next fall. Not wanting to lose this gal to higher education—as I had previously lost another gal—I suggested we buy a house together in Colorado Springs. I would join her for the winter, and we would both return to the ranch for the following summer. We found the perfect house, which helped to cement the enduring relationship we have today. We both felt marriage might ruin it all. Sadly, at that time many of our friends were getting divorced.

Meanwhile, life, adventures, and challenges were demanding and also a lot of fun. My philosophical focus had always been living on the edge, taking calculated risks, pushing the envelope of possibilities. We did all of that as the years flew by. Completing degrees in geology and climatology at CU's Colorado Springs campus, Amy took on the daunting role of managing a busy ranch, an expanding guide-outfitting business, education projects, and a growing international program.

Being pretty much finished with my earlier county jobs, I also sold my interest in the Arkansas River's first rafting company that friends and I had started some years back. Amy, Mike Lowe, and I started an adventure travel company/travel agency called Ultimate Escapes. This would be our structure for operating and marketing a growing number of programs based out of an old building in Colorado City, on the west side of Colorado Springs.

Meanwhile, summer activities continued to grow at the ranch. We were operating weekend adventures for several city parks and recreation departments from Colorado Springs, Aurora, and Westminster, along with educational field camps for Colorado College, UCCS, and Pueblo's growing campus.

Our ranch programs offered summer employment to numbers of interesting, talented young folk, college students, drifters, and more than a few overseas visitors with unquestioned visas. Those were more laid-back times. Nobody really cared in remote Custer County.

Several notable current residents got their Custer County start working at Bear Basin. Successful realtor Carolyn Abraham and her very capable mechanic husband, Bill, moved in to manage the operation when we were traveling or holed up in the city. Harold Frank arrived on horseback from New Mexico with his German army buddy Harry Sauter, bumping into Amy and me on a remote trail in the southern Wet Mountains. We invited them to visit us. They eventually took jobs wrangling at the ranch. Harry stayed on and became a Westcliffe builder for a number of years before moving on. Harold is still here, married to active local gal Lisa Frank.

Sometime during these busy years, French chef Stephan Guyonarg showed up on the scene. We had some fifteen seasonal employees and very much needed a cook. Trained in Paris, Stephan was our man. He stayed with us for several seasons and then went on to open a couple of now gone gourmet restaurants in Westcliffe with county resident Colleen Jorge. We remain in touch. Stephan is a neighbor, living close by on Highway 96.

Barbara Saint Amour was another amazing former ranch employee who remains in Westcliffe. She contributed immensely to local events and still can be found around the county playing music with local groups and entertaining at community gatherings and galas. She recently teamed up to play folksy gigs with another old friend and former Bear Basin wrangler, Linda Lorain. We continue to ride horses together and occasionally share an evening of fireside cowboy

**Barb, Linda, and Gary hammering out an oldie on
the ranch house porch**

music.

Buena Vista-based State Parks and Wildlife officer Kevin
Madler and his wife, Emily, met working on the ranch and
were married there. The list goes on and on. So many that I
have not mentioned have also contributed.

Good memories. A lingering appreciation haunts this nos-
talgic writing!

Meanwhile, I went back to pursuing cloud forest mysteries and lost ruins in Peru's high Andes several months each
year while Amy and the crew operated the ranch.

Between trips to Peru, adventures on the high seas, and
climbing, Amy and I continued to develop and operate related education programs at the ranch to help generate
needed income. Teaming up with British counsel Barry
Walker, we joined Cusco-based Manu Expeditions, dedicated
to Amazonian rain forest explorations and wildlife studies.
Later we formed Adventure Specialists Peru with Quechua-

speaking Cusco native Edwin Dueñas.

The company lives on today, dedicated to sponsoring archaeological explorations and quality adventure-educational programs. We maintain a stable of good horses there, which Edwin and crew use for custom trips to key Inca sites, finishing with narrated visits to Machu Picchu. Edwin has become an Inca expert over the years, serving as my research associate and logistical coordinator for our on-going Andean Research Project.

Building from my earlier anthropological work in Mexico's Sierra Madre with Colorado College and Outward Bound, we established educational trekking and later horse

**Gary and Edwin Dueñas on a remote Inca road
near Machu Picchu**

trips through the rugged canyons. We formed solid relationships with local mestizo families and indigenous Tarahumara ejidos (villages), which last to this day. We still have saddles, tents, and camping gear stashed there, although we no longer offer trips. Sadly, instability and associated violence in Pancho Villa's historic Chihuahua has made travel there inadvisable. Some there would like to see a return of Black Jack Pershing and maybe even the ghost of old Pancho to curb the anarchy.

Some years back, neighbor Hal Walter organized several Hardscrabble charity running events for the local San Isabel Foundation. I mention this because we brought in a team of Tarahumara runners with my old Sierra Madre contacts. It was amazing but sadly would likely not be possible today.

As years passed, beyond operating numerous multiple-day horseback trips in the Sanges and numerous guided climbs of the Crestone Peaks, we packaged up interesting programs in Argentina and Spain's Pyrenees.

We played polo in Argentina, learning to rope and ride gaucho-style. In the high Pyrenees, we explored old Roman

Gary and Amy exploring Spain's ancient Pyrenees

Joan and Robert Hamilton from Wetmore, with
Gary and Amy, playing polo in Argentina

Gary and a friend playing polo in Argentina

paths on spirited horses, staying in restored medieval castles
and twelfth century villas.

Numerous local friends joined us on those wild adventures. Amy and I, hosted by European-based former ranch

staff friends, used the opportunity to visit London, Paris, and horse shows in Italy. Luc Vincent, whose dad was then CEO of Scandinavian Airlines in Paris, furnished us with a sporty Mercedes to use as we toured western Europe. Luc continues to visit us for a few days out on horses each summer.

Our Peruvian partner, Edwin, has visited Bear Basin, as has my Royal Geological Society expedition partner Hugh Thomson. These amiable, welcome visits always bring positive events and memories to our now more isolated rural existence.

But now we have to move on to one of the prime formative events in the life Amy and I shared.

In the eventful century-turning year, 2000, we hosted a party at the ranch cowboy camp hidden away at a former aspen grove Ute campsite. Addressing assembled friends, adult beverages in hand, we announced that we planned to marry in ten years if we were still together. Between claps and groans, we enjoyed a gala campfire evening. Barb and I

Enjoying music at the ranch

whipped out the ranch version of Mike Burton's old "Night Ride's Lament," with Amy picking along on her 1930s Sovereign mandolin.

Packing in the Sangre de Cristo Mountains

Several changes and a major unfortunate event dominated the ensuing decade. First the positive events. I became an elected member of the coveted Pikes Peak Range Riders and served as their Ride Director during one demanding year, and we hosted their annual weeklong ride at the ranch in 2013. I continued to lecture on occasion at Colorado College and participated in other interesting activities in Colorado Springs, based from the old city house we still maintained.

I also became involved with NASA that year and guided a NASA group in Peru and lectured to astrophysicists at the Marshall Space Center. The topic was Andean geo-cosmic beliefs and related ceremonial structural alignments. Those were challenging and rewarding times.

Sometime during those years, we sold the Colorado riding/guiding business to old staffer friends, Dave and Michele Bennett, who still live on the ranch. Hard-riding/working Arkansas cowboy and cross-country trucker Mike Smithwick

Relaxing at the ranch

soon bought the business from them, running it as Bear Basin Pack Trips. We retained the riding and events business on the ranch while leasing shared ranch use to Mike. As time progressed, friends and former staffers Wes and Amy Phelps bought an interest in one of the ranch parcels, with plans to eventually build a summer cabin.

Key former ranch staff, Salida-based Dan Weiss and Kip Olson, stayed in touch helping with various projects as needed. Kip helped with cattle, horses, and caretaking needs when we were away. He remained a county resident with a small ranch southwest of the airport and a friendly gaited Paso Fino gelding called Smoke, kept here with our wild bunch.

But now for the unfortunate event. It happened late summer 2008. Amy and I eventually called the unfortunate event "different strokes for different folks."

We were sleeping, exhausted, in the old ranch bed, which

reputedly had belonged to Cripple Creek magnate Spenser Penrose. We had returned late from several days of camping and clearing trail up the middle fork of the Brush Creek canyons.

Amy suddenly fell out of bed.

A quick examination surprisingly suggested that she may have had a stroke. Thanks to a lightning-quick response from our county EMS unit, we soon had her down to the emergency room at Pueblo's Park View Hospital.

Diagnostics indicated she had probably suffered a massive ischemic right brain stroke that left her with no use of her left arm and a weakened left leg. The Pueblo docs did their best, but she is probably with us now thanks to immediate intervention from our old polo-playing and adventuring friend Dr. Robert Hamilton. We loaded her up in Robert's emergency-equipped Beechcraft King Air and flew her directly to the Mayo Clinic in Rochester, Minnesota. She recovered with the best care possible, but it was slow going.

Back in Colorado Springs, her recovery and therapy were slow and arduous. During that difficult time, life with Amy was an emotional roller coaster—up, down, and all around. We had a pouring in of help, support, and offers from friends, neighbors and organizations, which so positively typifies Custer County.

We struggled through the hard times, with Amy recouping what she could of her life and activities. With determination, we amazingly kept projects and the ranch rolling along, managing a trip or two to Peru and Mexico and our always exciting sailing getaways.

Amy took on a demanding project, documenting her experimental medical journey. She published her experiences in a well-received book entitled *Different Strokes for Different Folks.*

Time passed quickly. The year 2010 arrived uneventfully on a snowy, cold New Years morning:

Ten years ago on a bright Summer night
a man promised wedlock around a campfire light.
The ones who were there, they all agree
that the man who promised looked a lot like me

So we decided to do it, as the old proverb says, "for better or for worse." Whew! Planning and pulling off our big event would be a world class challenge. I have never been much for public celebrations, so the wedding would be a particular challenge for me. Fortunately, Amy was willing and now able to take on the lion's share of the logistics.

I started the adventure off by digging out an old emerald

Amy up on her Paso Fino, Sentinelo, several months after her stroke

from my South American memorabilia collection to make into a wedding ring.

A quick flashback to another time and life. I had acquired a small emerald collection from the black market in Bogota when traveling there for the Peace Corps. This was risky business. Exporting gems outside the official process was prohibited. The Colombian government quadrupled the cost, which went to graft and corruption. The black-market scam was to sell gems cheap and then assault or murder the purchaser shortly afterward to get them back.

My PC buddies had this figured out and knew how to avoid it, resulting in my getting the emeralds safely home. Selling them helped pay my college tuition. I kept one back for some special future occasion.

Amy's wedding ring

CHAPTER 16

Hee-Ha, Here Comes the Judge!
A Cowboy Wedding Remembered

Our wedding date, June 20, 2010, rolled around. We had long been planning what was probably to be the paramount event of our life and times together. Invitations were out; friends were coming from Peru, Spain, France, and assorted US states.

With a bit of philosophical reflection, I joked that we were throwing what traditional Native communities in Peru's remote Andes call an *ayllu raymi*. When a family or individuals reach a certain level of prosperity, they are obligated to throw a lavish party for the entity community. The tradition goes back to pre-Inca times as a means of annual redistribution of wealth. This event was indeed going to make a major dent in our less-than-excessive assets.

A general "y'all come" went out around the county. I sent out an open invite to members and families of the Pikes Peak

Range Riders, my active riding and western heritage events group. As Bill Monroe picked and sang in the 1950s: "When you live in the country / Everybody is your neighbor / On this one thing you can rely / They'll all come to see you. . . by and by."

We were then both active with the Sheriff's Department and the County's Search and Rescue unit. We were still a small, friendly, Old West community. Almost everyone knew each other and waved when passing on county roads. County officials, town and county employees, road and bridge workers, the fire department, the sheriff and commissioners were generally on courteous, friendly terms. A handshake and your word was still a bond and guarantee. So that was the way it was in the not-too-distant past. We knew almost everyone. Many came to the wedding.

We sent out a few formal invites to close friends and left an open invitation to anyone who wanted to join in. All were welcome, and boy did they come. We planned for around two

Sign directing guests to our wedding

hundred. More than 350 showed up. Thanks to exceptionally helpful friends and Amy's management, it all came off smoothly, and we easily accommodated the expanded numbers of guests.

Amy and her team diligently made the arrangements. We were locating the festivities and ceremony at Bear Basin's Cowboy Camp, one of the ranch's special wilderness hideaways. We had placed the camp amidst ancient shaped and carved ponderosa pine surrounded by even older aspen groves. Years later, during local archaeological investigations, I determined that the location was one of a number of ceremonial sites situated around the ranch lands. Bear Basin had been utilized as a summer camping and sacred center for a band of Utes associated with Pikes Peak (Tava), their primary terrestrial spirit. It is interesting that we chose to place the camp at this special location long before I became aware of its cultural significance. There may be more to spiritual places than science understands.

Moving on to the big event. Out-of-town invitees included Reidun Johansson, a relative of Norwegian Arctic explorer Roald Amundsen, a good friend and former guide, flew in from Spain. Mark Trockman, professional photographer and veteran of our Peru and Sierra Madre trips, cheerfully showed up, camera and lenses in hand. Our old French cowboy friend and Europe touring partner Luc Vincent arrived from Paris.

Talented, Pueblo-based folk-country musician Tom Munch and the energized "Atomic Fire Balls" band were onboard to provide proper cowboy music, which indeed they did! Local crooners and pickers Guy Madden and Drew Horton arrived, instruments in hand. My old "Chet Atkins" J-50 Gibson somehow showed up in the mix. Just maybe, after a second margarita, I could join in on the coming jam?

Gary joined the band for a couple of songs

The ranch crew had set up a huge circus-sized tent and a large, moved by sections, dance floor. This had been a logistical problem solved by a generous loaned platform from the Custer County Cattlewomen. A large flat area nearby, at Dry Lake, was designated for parking. Guests either walked over to the tent area or rode in on an arranged shuttle vehicle.

The big resident yurt at the camp was set up as kitchen and staging facially. A local catering company prepared huge amounts of beef, chicken, vegetables, and desserts. Several volunteers generously tended bar.

The band tuned up. Guests were seated or grouped about. The stage was set.

"Here comes the Judge."

Old Saddle Club friend and county judge Peter Michael-

Amy and Gary rode horses to the wedding

son rode in, black robes streaming, on his big buckskin gelding. Amy and I showed up shortly after, she riding her favorite gaited Paso Fino, Sentinelo, I on my favorite quarter horse
mare, Zippa. Passing the horses to handlers, we strolled into
the tent hand-in-hand.

Tom and the boys stuck up a rousing version of Richard
Wagner's old operatic favorite "Here Comes the Bride" as the
crowd clapped and cameras clicked. Standing solemnly before Pete, we listened as he read off the state-prescribed lan-
guage the ceremony required. We staged a planned hesitation
to the ceremonial "Do you take,—" which the crowd loved,

Yorick, the presenter of the rings

and then reluctantly agreed. Pete cheerfully pronounced us man and wife.

Another helpful friend, Jay Rhodemiyer, set free the ring bearer. Great Dane Yorick bounced up on the stage as rehearsed and presented our rings that were attached to his collar. The crowd went wild!

Let the festivities begin.

Friend forever, former Bear Basin wrangler, and world class musician Barbara St. Amour played and sang two of our favorites: "The Campfire Waltz" and "Together Strong." We were allowed the first dance alone and then were joined by a multitude as the band took over the entertainment.

Sometime after a near gourmet feeding frenzy and enhancing libations, Drew, Guy, and I joined the band, hammering out favorite old ranch songs.

The festivities went on and on into the warm summer night, continuing onward to these present challenging and different times.

When the moon rises over Bear Peak and the coyotes roam and sing, you can hear the old guitars ring.

CHAPTER 17

The Road to Ruins—Inca Ruins

I returned to Andean expeditions and archaeological explorations in the 1980s. Associates and I began opening old Inca routes and surveying seldom-visited Inca sites. A primary interest had always been the mystery of Choquequirao, a late Inca site we believe was modeled after Machu Picchu. University of Colorado archaeo-astronomer J. McKim Malville and I published a book about the complex and our related work at Machu Picchu: *Machu Picchu's*

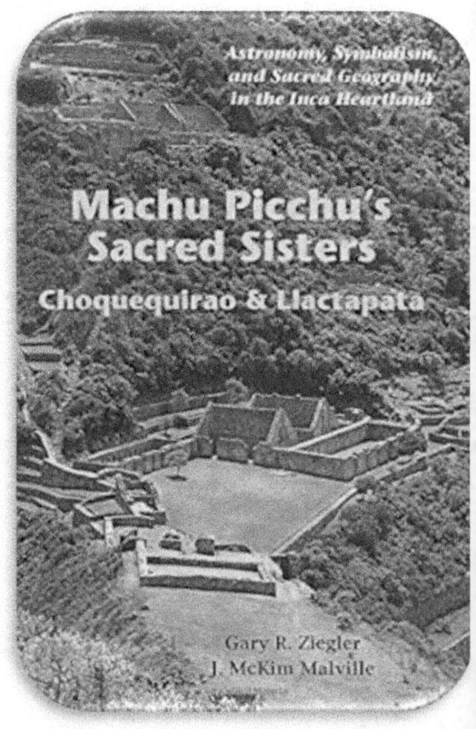

Sacred Sisters: Choquequirao and Llactapata—Astronomy, Symbolism, and Sacred Geography in the Inca Heartland.

After we opened up the abandoned Inca route to Choquequirao from Vilcabamba, I teamed up with Cusco archaeologist Percy Paz, intermittently working there over the next decade or so. Meanwhile, our various projects poked around all of the principal sites from Cusco to the lower Apurimac.

In 1990, Amy and I formed a company called Adventure Specialists, specializing in educational adventures on horseback and foot in Colorado and Peru. The following is a trip report from our 2018 Andean Research project.

"Steve, bail out, I shouted!" Horrified, I watched helplessly as his bay horse slid off the narrow, muddy track, flipping upside down, legs flailing into the deep ichu grass-lined gully.

Steve Lasswell, team member and at the time mayor of Silver Cliff, managed an athletic tuck and roll, clearing the struggling horse as they landed together unharmed in dense polylepis growth below. Both were soon retrieved with some difficulty by machetes and ropes. We wisely decided it was time for a break.

"Steve, you just qualified for an army airborne badge," I quipped, as we popped open a couple of Power Bars.

The ancient cloud forest Inca trail we were following had not been cleared or used in decades. Deep groves and remains of old chopped trunks indicated that it had probably seen travel in the past, post-Inca times, by local herders, but it had long fallen out of use and memory.

My Cusco-based research associate and expedition *maestre-de-campo* Edwin Dueñas, along with our long-time head wrangler, *arriero*, Pio Espinosa, had previously scouted out the route on a planning reconnaissance.

They reported sightings of mountaintop ruins and thought that we would be able to open and follow the old Inca route to get near them. We calculated that with extensive clearing, helped by a local crew from the nearby Santa Teresa Valley, we could then drop down to the spot where we had terminated previous explorations in 2016. That area had an access road leading back to civilization.

This was the latest in a series of annual exploratory expeditions that a small group of us had been undertaking since our 2003 rediscovery and surveying of the what we called "Machu Picchu's ceremonial neighbor," the extensive archaeological complex of Llactapata.

Located less than five kilometers distant, and several hours travel time away from Machu Picchu during Inca occupation, Llactapata was a busy complex of separate but interconnected areas: ceremonial features, *huacas*, temples, *usnus*, a water-focused sector, and a large urban agricultural district supporting the now famous estate of Pachacuti: the royal builder of Machu Picchu.

American explorer Hiram Bingham found part of the Llactapata site in 1912. It soon became overgrown. Our 2003-2005 explorations uncovered an extensive complex on a ridge and hillside covering several square kilometers facing Machu Picchu. We located, cleared, and diagramed several hundred structures, which we organized into five sectors. Our group, led by Hugh Thomson and I, included Kim Malville, John Leivers, old Peace Corps friend Jack Vetter, Nick Asheshov, Amy Finger Ziegler, and a talented field team. The expedition was supported by the Royal Geographical Society of London and its former director John Hemming. John is considered the world's leading authority on the Inca conquest. We also carried a historic Explorers Club flag. A most exciting discovery was locating the main Inca road connecting Machu Picchu with distant Vilcabamba and Choquequirao.

We documented our exploration of the steep, dense cloud-forest slopes and the subsequent locating and surveying of lost ruins, with discovery of the Inca trail to Machu Picchu's Hanging Bridge. This is reported in our field report (J. Malville, H. Thomson, and G. Ziegler, "The Road to Ruins," Revista Andina 39 [2004]). The original field report was published in Peru's professional journal in Spanish.

The Llactapata sites are located lower down, on a long multi-summited ridge running southward up to the glacier-covered roof of 20,500-foot Salkantay, the highest peak in the

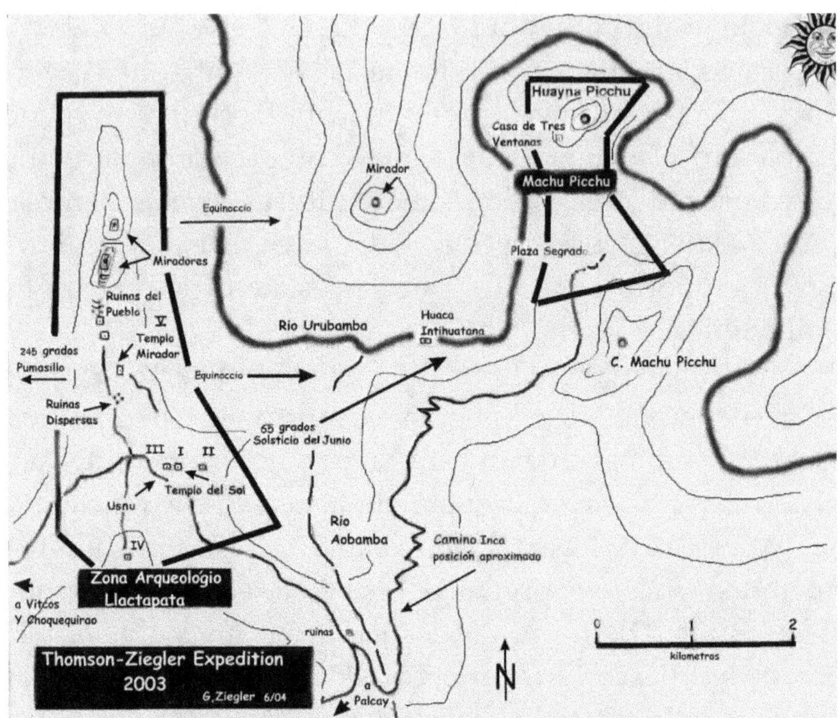

Map showing the location of Llactapata in
relationship to Machu Picchu

Vilcabamba range. The Machu Picchu complex is situated on
a parallel ridge, separated from the Llactapata ridge by the
deep canyon of the Aobamba River.

A steep, geologically unstable mixture of fractured granite plutons, folded and faulted down-trending metamorphic
strata, unstable colluvium breakdown, and high glacial mo-
raine, creates a hostile and dangerous landscape here. Recent catastrophic slides and flooding have tragically
demonstrated this.

In 1998, an El Nino year, a massive flood occurred after the
Aobamba Canyon was dammed by a huge ice slide breaking
away from Salkantay. When the massive backed-up lake and
debris eventually broke free, it plunged down to block and
flood the Urubamba River and canyon below.

Hundreds were killed as the flooding swept away river-side towns, bridges, and the railroad. The rails were never replaced. Now the rail line terminates at the hydroelectric plant eleven kilometers below Machu Picchu.

I trekked through the devastated area several months later, penning a short story from an eyewitness, which I titled "The Last Train to Quillabamba." Here is some of what I wrote at the time:

Mule trails are wiped out and just now being reopened. The railroad to Quillabamba is gone from the hydroelectric plant (so is the plant) about ten kilometers below Machu Picchu. A tremendous flood came down the Quebrada Aobamba (the next side canyon downriver from Machu Picchu), damming up the Urubamba, filling the valley with a broad, long lake that covers the plant.

At the time, the railroad stopped at the first switchback above the lake and the rails disappeared into the water. My photo taken from high above the canyon with Machu Picchu in the background looks like a Norwegian fjord. Tourists, and even most Cusco residents, were unaware of this area, as it was not visible from Machu Picchu or from the tourist trains that stop at Puente Ruinas, well upriver.

Accounts of personal hardships and tragedy are everywhere. An engine and several cars sit abandoned on a short section of rails terminated on either end by the river.

A woman told me an incredible story. She had just boarded the train from Santa Teresa at 3:30 p.m. on February 27 on its way to Machu Picchu and Cusco when the train suddenly stopped in a torrential rain. The crew forced everyone off the train and up the steep canyon side. Moments later, the train was swept away, never to be found.

In 2006, we hiked down the massively eroded Aobamba Canyon, following what remained of an old Inca road. But now I must go back to the present expedition.

April weather in the high Andes is never completely predictable. The intensity of the rainy season usually slacks by late March, allowing reasonably comfortable, landslide-free travel. Anomalies like El Nino contribute uncertainty to an already uncertain science.

We were soon to experience some of the worst of that uncertainty. Fog, mist, rain, and deep mud made the trails treacherous and trying. Travel was arduous. Several of our camps were almost bivouacs, chopped out of steep slopes at fourteen thousand feet or more. Comfortable dry tents, our chef Pancho's near gourmet meals, and the evening ration of single-malt libations helped make it all bearable. Of course, and most important, was the successful achievement of our objectives.

Before launching the expedition, seven of us, along with an old friend, David Espejo, met for a traditional happy hour briefing at Cusco's Norton's Pub. David goes way back with me to the early Vilcabamba expeditions.

Getting through the needed logistics, David and I began telling old stories of places, events and adventures we had shared. One of the best being an Australian feature-length fantasy film, *Lost City of Gold*, which we had starred in together. He had played a coca-leaf-chewing mystical Andean shaman and I a dour Hiram Bingham-like character. Sadly, he could not join us on this expedition.

Early out on the road the next morning, we had time to visit Quillarumiyoc, one of my favorite Inca sites along the

Quillarumiyoc—"place of the moon rock"

central highway heading west toward the Apurimac. Previously, I had helped interpret the extensive number of features as a multi-ceremonial complex.

It is spread over several square kilometers on a gentle sloping hillside encompassing rounded hills and a lush wet valley. The geological structure is a gray limestone, similar to much of the base rock of Cusco. It is soft, uniform in consistency, and easily shaped.

Quillarumiyoc is a Disneyland of sacred landscapes, objects, *huacas*, manipulation of water, and geo-cosmic alignment. It seems to incorporate most of the important elements of traditional Andean spiritualism along with important solstice focus.

There is a cave with fine masonry inside, like the Cave of the Moon at Machu Picchu. There are a number of large sculpted boulders, like the White Rock at Vitcos and Yuroc Rumi, which probably replicated the surrounding topography.

Gary in front of the upright monolith at Quillarumiyoc

There is a channeled stream complete with a waterfall into a stone-lined pool. There are petroglyphs and carved seats that face the December solstice sunrise and the June solstice sunset. There are also stepped *usnu* (platforms) with paved walkways and steps.

The *pièce de résistance* is a raised and filled U-shaped *usnu* enclosed by a carefully made retaining wall of imported square-shaped and reddish andesite blocks. The open end of the U faces north, ending with a giant shaped boulder as the backdrop.

The centerpiece of the platform facing the boulder is a tall upright monolith carved in a traditional stepped motif, which Kim Malville suggests is a symbolic stairway to Hanan Pacha, the world above.

Another unique feature is a stylized half circle carved in the steep side of one of the large boulders—large enough for two or more to sit in. A hole in the floor allows offertory fluids to flow out some distance below. The outward alignment is 110 degrees, facing the December solstice sunrise on the near horizon.

This is the best-known feature and the reason for the name given to the site. *Quilla* means "moon" in Quechua. Early visitors thought the carving represented the moon.

That afternoon we drove on to camp near Lima Tambo. Tents were set up, gear was sorted from the van and preparations were made for a horse-mounted departure the next morning.

After crossing several high passes, we reached a previous campsite at Hiram Bingham's remote site, Palcay, two days later. During a break from work at Machu Picchu in 1912, Bingham visited and sketched a plan for this then undocumented site.

Located in a deep canyon near the upper limit of the

A wrangler looking across the valley toward the Palcay site

Aobamba River, Palcay is extremely difficult to reach. Decades later, in 1985, American anthropologist and mountaineer Johan Reinhard visited Palcay. He described Palcay and another lost Inca site located between it and the upper reaches of the Llactapata archaeological zone. British archaeo-explorer Hugh Thomson also explored the region in the 1980s while working with the British archaeologist Ann Kindall on her Cusichaca project.

In 2006, our expedition reached Palcay after a long, difficult backpacking slog up from the Santa Teresa Valley to the West. I published "Palcay, an Almost Lost City and Other Explorations: A Report of the 2006 Andean Research Expedition" in *South American Explorer*, # 84 in 2007. An excerpt explains our objective:

Our immediate goal was to reach Palcay to survey and interpret the site. We hoped to visit two other small ruins reported by Reinhard and definitively locate the several Inca roads known to have passed through the region. We would look for other Inca or pre-Inca constructions to complete the reconnaissance. As the region is so difficult to access, we probably would not return again. We must give it our best shot.

Expeditioning in the Andes requires tremendous planning, time, and funding. Each season, we are usually able to accomplish only one exploration, resulting in that we plan and choose very carefully where we explore each year. My own focus over the past several decades had been systematically investigating likely locations for Inca activity in the Vilcabamba which now receives a lower priority. Since our exciting 2003 discovery at Llactapata, along with the realization that a complex design relationship of ceremonial sites surround and were associated with Machu Picchu, we have concentrated efforts to gather all the related data we can.

We hope to better understand what I call Machu Picchu's geo-cosmic grid of shrines, *huacas*, sacred mountains, *apus*, celestial, and in particular, solstice-equinox alignments. Ongoing Llactapata-Machu Picchu studies strongly suggest that all the regional sites and the numerous viewing platforms, *usnus*, are laid out by placement and design in planned relationship to each other, important terrain features and astronomical alignments. We were eager to see if, or how, Palcay and the high Aobamba sites would fit this model.

So, here we were again some twelve years later. Unfortunately, none of the 2006 team could be with us. John Leivers was happily training a ladies rowing team in Australia. John Martin, most recently with us on the October 2016 project, had committed to a family journey to Easter Island. Paolo Greer was involved in other projects but as always was on email standby to send a collage of satellite images upon our return.

Our new team had two project veterans: Steve Lasswell, an intrepid expeditionary veteran, and Quechua-speaking Jack Vetter, who first signed on for the 2003 Llactapata investigations. Jack had made almost every annual exploration there since. Three new enthusiastic others rounded out the team along with Edwin, Pio, camp chef Pancho, and me.

George Koons, a Colorado friend, was a skilled, fit, back country horseman and adventurer who we successfully talked into joining on. Bill Tollard—a friend of Mark and Jim Johnson from Denver, who had been members of the April 2016 Research Expedition to Incaracay and Choquequirao—signed on with their encouragement. Having poked around remote Alaska, Bill was well prepared.

The third new member, Kevin Miller, was a young educated adventurer, eager to learn and carry on professional explorations in the remote Andes. I suspected he may have accumulated more than enough experience with the mud, rain, and extremes we encountered. His "got to get up there" attitude reminds me of a younger John Leivers forcing us to climb the highest rocky knob summits at Llactapata or chop through where none dared go.

Although it was well off the tourist circuit, when we arrived at Palcay I had expected to see the area cleared and at least partially restored and protected. It appeared as if it had not been touched since our last visit. Walls were crumbling; cattle had been inside the structures; vines, moss, and shrubs

had reclaimed much of what we previously had documented.

The only sign of official activity was a small cement monument with a brass plate stating, "This is a protected archaeological site in the Machu Picchu Park."

Protected by whom and how we wondered?

However, some changes had happened. An elderly lady Hugh Thomson had met there many years back greeted us upon arrival. She asked for payment and complained that we had damaged the trail down from the pass. She said that she planned to put up a locked gate on the pass to prevent such intrusion.

After lengthy dialogue in Quechua and the exchange of several hundred soles, Peru's currency, the problem was resolved. We were free to camp and conduct our investigations.

Yet another surprise awaited us. I was told, "Jefe, hay un

gringo viviendo aqui" (Boss, there is a foreigner living here). Soon, an amiable American from upstate New York arrived at our camp, introducing himself as Nate. He had been living here for some time, involved with various studies and projects, which we did not probe into.

An item that caught my immediate attention was the mention of more ruins on the other side of the Aobamba River, including a stone monument with incised petroglyphs that Nate had found. Unfortunately, we were short on time, scheduled to move out the next morning for the long slog up to investigate our primary objective, the ridge top sites far in the distance above us.

Kevin immediately volunteered to accompany Nate and cross the intimidating swift torrent for a quick recon of what might be there. The next morning, I briefed them on collecting details and loaned them my Brunton surveying compass. Off they went while we packed up camp.

Apparently there was a ceremonial aspect to Palcay, which we had suspected but failed to find in 2006. Nate and Kevin's quick probe seemed to substantiate this. I regretted that our schedule could not permit another day there. Anyway, we now had a solid reason to return. Fortunately, Kevin returned with several photos and a description of what we called Palcay Sector II.

With the group reassembled, we left Palcay behind. As it turned out, we also left the last comfortable camp. We followed a good trail across the big side canyon coming down from Salcantay, ending up at a small potato farm and Nate's cabin. From there, the trail abruptly ended.

Climbing steeply upward, the overgrown remnant of an

old Inca trail headed diagonally up. We expected tough going, but nothing like what we encountered. We had hiked
down a part of this trail in 2006 with backpacks, not with a
string of saddle horses and pack mules. We took turns up
front swinging machetes while slogging through deep mud.
As we climbed, Edwin reassuringly said, "Guys, it will go
through. We did this last year on the recon. Not to worry."

Despite Edwin's assurances, we did have growing con-
cerns. At the start, we had to cross a swiftly flowing stream of
knee-deep cold water, which filled boots. The soles of my su-
per-tech "waterproof" new boots had already come apart and
were now secured by duct tape.

As light rain and fog settled in for the remaining days of
the expedition, the boots were never dry. Most of our other
waterlogged gear also remained wet. Fortunately, sleeping
gear and spare clothes stayed dry in bags on the pack mules. It
was during the next several days travel that Steve's horse fell
off the trail. Several other "unfortunate incidents" occurred,

luckily all without injury.

It was difficult to travel with massive washouts and a trail passible only by foot. Apparently, there has been no interest in reopening it. The high boggy cloud forest trail we were now climbing was certainly not used by anyone. Along the way we located and surveyed a large ceremonial group with a mountain top *usnu* called Mishihuayunca, which translates to "place of the dead cat." We hoped to learn how these last undocumented sites might have had been associated with ceremonial activities at Machu Picchu and Llactapata.

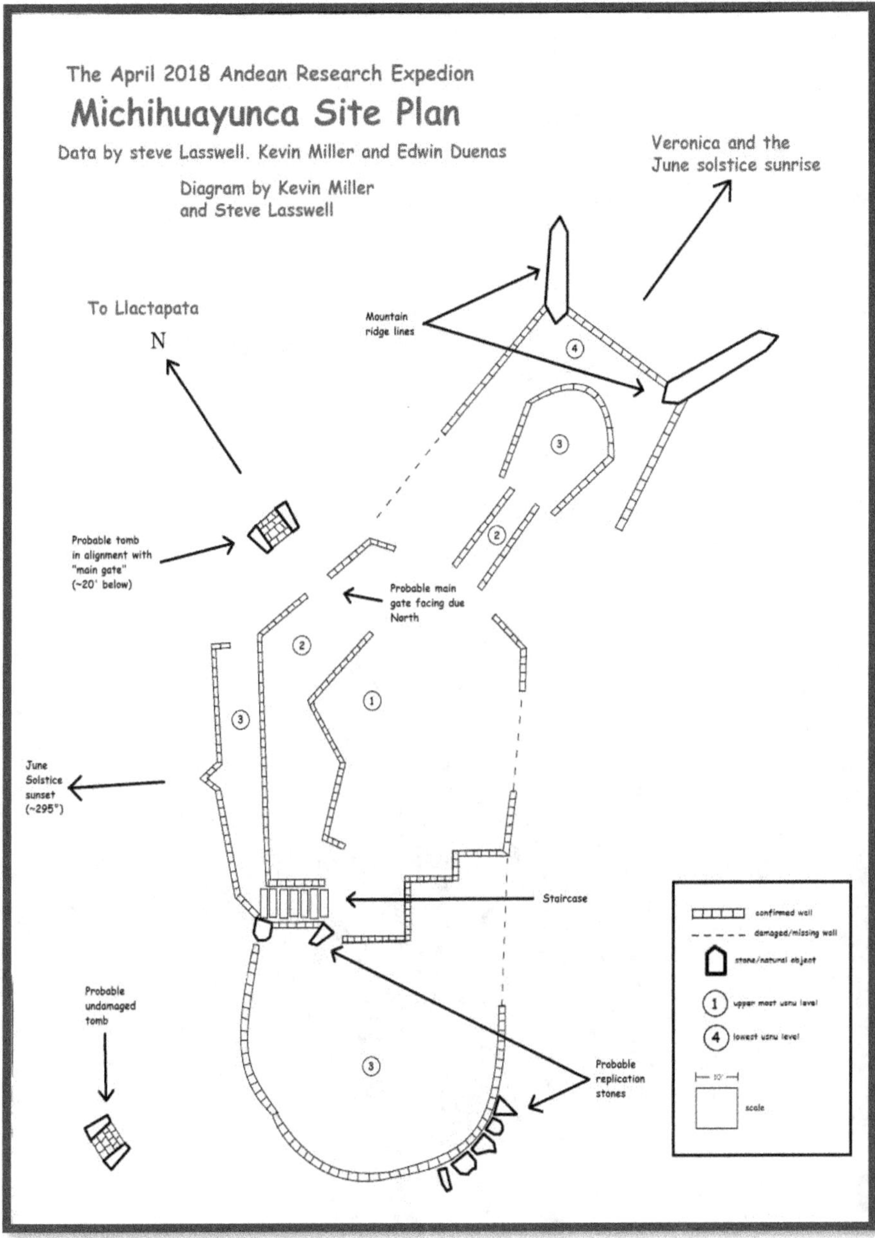
The April 2018 Andean Research Expedion
Michihuayunca Site Plan
Data by steve Lasswell. Kevin Miller and Edwin Duenas
Diagram by Kevin Miller
and Steve Lasswell
To Llactapata
N
Veronica and the
June solstice sunrise
Mountain
ridge lines
4
3
2
Probable tomb
in alignment with
"main gate"
(~20' below)
Probable main
gate facing due
North
2
1
3
June
Solstice
sunset
(~295°)
Staircase
Probable
undamaged
tomb
3
Probable
replication
stones
confirmed wall
damaged/missing wall
stone/natural object
1   upper most usnu level
4   lowest usnu level
10'
scale

During a lunch break, Pio managed to get the pack string around us and out in front. Late in the day, we stumbled exhausted, soaked, and caked in mud into a high grassy basin with tents up and waiting.

Pio's wranglers had accomplished the impossible. They struggled all day with the animals, mud, packing, and unpacking and still managed to have camp set up for our arrival. They were the best! Steve's GPS said we were at 12,900 feet.

I pulled my large, yellow river bag into the tent and zipped up the door. A plastic tarp was inside to keep items dry from the floor, which always bleeds moisture up from the ground. We had brought long-used inflatable waterproof sleeping pads, so unless something touched the side of the tent, items that arrived dry stayed dry.

Changing into warm fleece, I tossed my mud-covered soggy boots outside, leaving them out in the rain. Maybe it would wash off the mud? I pulled on a pair of neoprene dive boots and sloshed over to the big dining tent.

Bill and Jack were already at the table munching quesadillas and popcorn. All of us soon arrived. Edwin appeared with a bottle of Johnny Walker Black to complement the hot tea and rapidly disappearing snacks.

It was amazing how fast we all came back to life. Hardships were forgotten with a good dose of comforts and conversation. The talk stopped immediately when plates heaped with fried chicken and mashed potatoes arrived. We finished eating and were soon back in our individual tents. We were all tired, but we knew after a long night of comfortable rest, another adventure in Peru's high country awaited us.

Who knew what roads we would follow tomorrow and what ruins we might find.

The End
Until we meet again around a campfire.

Bibliography

Books and Articles

Bauer, Brain S., Halac-Higashimori, Madeleine, and Cantarutti, Gabriel E. *Voices from Vilcabamba*, Boulder CO: University of Colorado Press, 2016.

Bauer, Brian S., Santa Cruz, Javier Fonseca, and Solva, Miriam Aráoz. *Vilcabamba and the Archaeology of Inca Resistance*, Albuquerque, NM: University of New Mexico Press, 2015.

Bingham, Hiram. *Lost City of the Incas*, Introduction by Hugh Thomson, London: Weidenfeld & Nicolson, 2001.

Blair, Laurence. "Peru's last Inca city reveals its secrets: 'It's genuinely a marvel," *The Guardian*, September 28, 2018.

"Colorado College Students Splurge, Spend $60 On 11-Day Trip to Mexico," *The Catalyst*, undated.

D'Altroy, Terence. *The Incas*, London: Blackwell Publishing, 2003.

Davis, David G. "No Old Gold or Bones? A Skeptical Review of "Caverna del Oro" Legend", *The Journal of Spelean History*, October-Decemeber, 1993, https://caves.org/wp-content/uploads/Publications/journal-of-spelean-history/092.pdf.

Edwards, Jr., Fred L. *The Bridges of Vietnam: From the Journals of a U.S. Marine Intelligence Officer* Denton, TX: University of Texas, 2000), https://archive.org/details/bridgesofvietnam0000edwa.

Fall, Bernard B. *Streets without Joy: Indochina at War; 1946-1954*, Mechanicsburg, PA: Stackpole Books, 1961.

Halberstam, David. *The Best and the Brightest*, New York, NY: Ballantine Books, 1993.

Hemming, John. *The Conquest of the Incas*, London: Pan-Macmillan, 1970, 1993 (revised).

Herring, George. *America's Longest War: The United States and Vietnam, 1950-1975*, Hoboken, NJ: John Wiley & Sons, Inc., 1979.

Hyslop, John. *The Inca Road System*, New York, NY: Academic Press, 1984.

Lanning, Edward P. *Peru before the Incas*, Englewood Cliffs, New Jersey: Prentice-Hall, Inc., 1967, Peru before the Incas : Lanning, Edward P : Free Download, Borrow, and Streaming : Internet Archive.

Lee, Vincent. *Forgotten Vilcabamba: Final Stronghold of the Inca*, San Francisco, CA: Empire Publishing, 2000.

Lindsey, David A., Andrienssen, P. A. M., and Wirdlaw, Bruce R. "Heating, Cooling and Uplift during Tertiary Time, Northern Sangre de Cristo Range, Colorado," *Geological Society of America Bulletin*, Volume 97, 1133-1143.

MacDonald, Charles B. and Charles V.P. von Luttichau, Charles V. P. *American Military History*, "Chapter 28: The U.S. Army in Vietnam," Center of Military History, United States Army, 1969.

MacQuarrie, Kim. *The Last Days of the Inca*, New York, NY: Simon & Shuster, 2007.

Malville, J. McKim; Thomson, Hugh; Ziegler, Gary. "'El redescubrimiento de Llactapata, antiguo observatorio de Machu Picchu," *Revista Andina* (2004 #39), Translated as "Machu Picchu's Observatory: The Re-Discovery of Llactapata and its Sun-Temple."

Marshall-Sprague. *Newport in the Rockies: The Life & Good Times of Colorado Springs*, Colorado Springs, CO: Swallow Press, 1988.

Martin, Douglas. "Gene Savoy, Flamboyant Explorer of Ruins, Dies at 80," September 19, 2007, *New York Times*, Gene Savoy, Flamboyant Explorer of Ruins, Dies at 80 - The New York Times (nytimes.com).

Reinhard, Johan. *Informe sobre una sección del camio Inca y las ruinas en la crestaque baja del Nevado de Tucharhuay entre los rios Aobamba y Santa Teresa*, Revista Sacsahuaman, no. 3:163-187, Cusco, 1990.

Savoy, Gene. *Antisuyo, The Search for the Lost Cities of the Amazon*, New York, NY: Simon & Schuster, 1970.

Sheehan, Niel. *A Bright Shining Lie: John Paul Vann and America in Vietnam*, New York, NY: Vintage Books, 1989.

Stewart, Richard W., Editor. *American Military History, Volume II, The United States Army in the Global Era*, Army History Series, Chapter 28.

Thomson, Hugh. *Cochineal Red: Travels through Ancient Peru*, London: Weidenfeld & Nicolson, 2007.

Thomson, Hugh. *The White Rock: An Exploration of the Inca Heartland*, London: Weidenfeld & Nicolson, 2001.

Tuchman, Barbara. *The March of Folly: From Troy to Vietnam*, New York, NY: Penguin Random House, 1985.

Ziegler, Gary. "From Spanish Conquistadors to hidden gold, local archeologist untangles the truth from myths of the Marble Mountain Caves in the Sangre de Cristo Mountains," *Wet Mountain Tribune*, November 28, 2024.

Ziegler, Gary. "Vilcabamba, Report from the Field," *South American Explorer*, vol. 57, 1999.

Ziegler, Gary R.; Malville, J. McKim; Ruggles, Clive ed. "Choquequirao, Topa Inca's Machu Picchu: A Royal Estate and Ceremonial Center," *Archeoastronomy and Ethnoastronomy: Building Bridges Between Cultures*, Oxford IX International Symposium on Archeoastronomy, Cambridge: Cambridge University Press, 2011.

Ziegler, Gary R.; Malville, J. McKim. *Machu Picchu's Sacred Sisters: Choquequirao & Llactapata*, Boulder, CO: Johnson Books, 2013.

Zuidema, R. Tom. *The Ceque System in Cuzco: The Social Organization of the Capital of the Inca*, Leiden: E. J. Brill, 1964.

Websites

"Chimborazo," Wikipedia: The Free Encyclopedia,
    https://en.wikipedia.org/wiki/Chimborazo.
"Crestone Needle," Wikipedia: The Free Encyclopedia,
    https://en.wikipedia.org/wiki/Crestone_Needle.
"David Ziegler," Wikipedia: The Free Encyclopedia,
    https://en.wikipedia.org/wiki/David_Ziegler.
"Johan Reinhard," Wikipedia: The Free Encyclopedia, Johan
    Reinhard - Wikiwand.
"Jorge C. Muelle," Wikipedia: The Free Encyclopedia, Jorge C.
    Muelle - Wikipedia, la enciclopedia libre.
"Luis Guillermo Lumbreras," Wikipedia: The Free Encyclope-
    dia, Luis Guillermo Lumbreras - Wikipedia.
"Universidad Nacional Mayor de San Marcos," Top Universi-
    ties, Universidad Nacional Mayor de San Marcos : Rank-
    ings, Fees & Courses Details | Top Universities.
"The Vietnam War," U.S. Army Center of Military History,
    https://history.army.mil/index.html.

About the Author

Gary Ziegler is a field archaeologist with a geology background, a mountaineer, an explorer, and the owner of Custer County's Bear Basin Ranch. He has spent nearly a lifetime climbing mountains, exploring Custer County, and studying remote Inca sites in Peru's Southern Andes. He is a fellow of the Royal Geographical Society and the Explorers Club. He has been featured in documentary films from the BBC, the Discovery Channel, the Science Channel, and the History Channels.

In 2013, he was awarded the Distinguished Lecturer title at NASA's Marshal Space Center. He has taught at Colorado College and Peru's national university in San Marcos. His home base is the four-thousand-acre Bear Basin Ranch in the Sangre de Cristo Mountains of southern Colorado's Custer County, where he formerly served as sheriff and founder of the search and rescue unit.

Index